BONHAM

southbank
publishing

JOHN
BONHAM

The Powerhouse Behind Led Zeppelin

Mick Bonham

First published in 2005
Southbank Publishing
P O Box 394, Harpenden,
Herts, AL5 1XJ

A CIP catalogue record for this book is available from the British Library.

ISBN: 978 1 904915 11 9

Edited by Phil Richards

Additional material © Phil Richards

Photographs in this book are from the Mick Bonham archives in association with Icarus Publications, with additional images courtesy of Michael Putland at Retna Pictures, the Howard Mylett Collection and Rex Features Limited. Additionally the photograph on page 28 is by M. Randolf.

We deeply regret it, if, despite our efforts, any copyright owners have been unintentionally overlooked and omitted. We will amend any such errors in the next edition if they are brought to the attention of the publisher.

6 8 10 9 7

Typeset by Avocet Typeset, Chilton, Aylesbury, Bucks
Printed and bound by CPI Group (UK) Ltd, Croydon, CR0 4YY

With thanks to all those who took part
in the writing of this book.

For Dennis and Debbie
without whom none of it would have been possible.

Contents

Foreword

About ten years ago, after reading yet another load of rubbish about his brother John, my husband Mick turned to me and said, "I should write a book about 'our kid', if only to tell Zoe (John's daughter) what a great bloke her dad was." And with that the seeds of this book began to grow.

Mick was not a writer, he wrote as he spoke and when I read his book I can still hear him and feel his wicked sense of humour. I hope you will be able to share that too. As you read on, it becomes clear that John was not only his brother and friend, but also his hero, and when John died a large gap was left in Mick's life and until his own untimely death, no one would ever fill it.

Those who are close to our family will realise that Mick writes of a lighter side to life, he left a lot of memories untold as they were either private, personal or too painful, i.e. his description of John's death is brief, he could not find the words to measure his pain.

Mick died suddenly on 14 January 2000, aged 49. He had just completed the first re-write, but I guess it would have had several if time had allowed. However, we all felt that the book should be printed basically as he wrote it, so that his humour and character could be felt throughout. I hope you enjoy sharing their life together as Mick saw it.

This book is a tribute to two heroes, one of Mick's and one of mine...

Linda Bonham
September 2005

Opposite
Mick Bonham

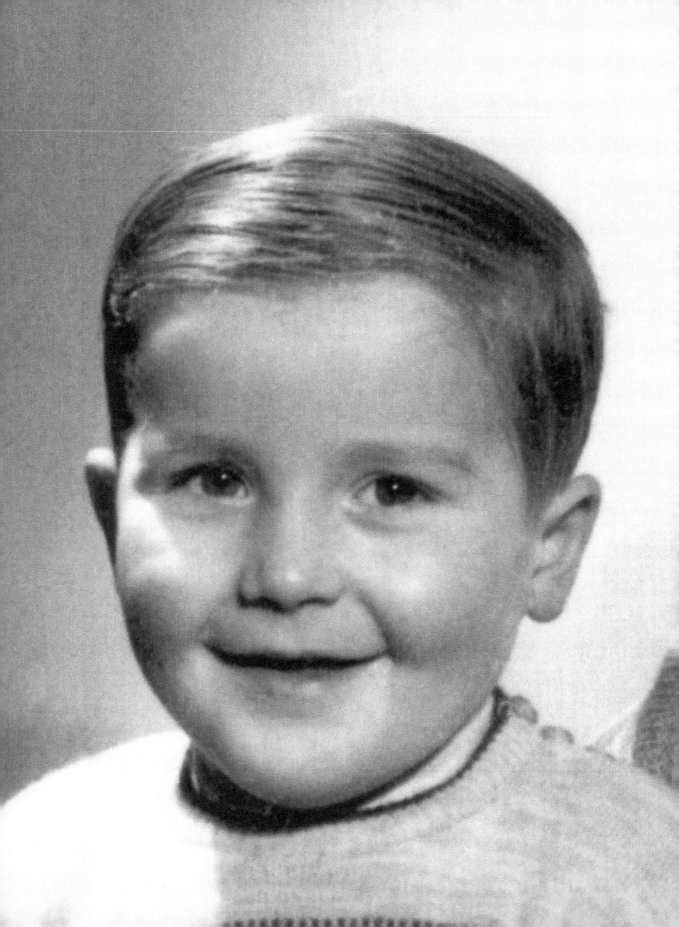

Chapter 1

IN THE DAYS OF MY YOUTH

"I've wanted to be a drummer since I was about five years old. I used to play on a bath salt container with wires on the bottom, and on a round coffee tin with a loose wire fixed to it to give a snare drum effect. Plus there were always my Mum's pots and pans. When I was ten, my Mum bought me a snare drum. My Dad bought me my first full drum kit when I was 15. It was almost prehistoric. Most of it was rust."
– John Bonham

My brother John was born with an extremely enlarged and bruised cranium, following twenty-six hours of labour, unfortunately for our Mum (Joan). He entered the world weighing in at a grand ten pounds four ounces.

He was named after our Dad, John Henry, who for some unknown reason was called Jacko by everyone.

Home was a nice three bedroom semi-detached house on the outskirts of Redditch, which is about 20 miles from Brum, in a village called Hunt End. John Henry Jr. was two years older than me, and this angelic looking little lad would take me on some great nights, and get me into some hard fights.

As the first few years passed, I noticed that John had a passion for hitting things – biscuit tins, sweet boxes and anything else that made a sound. What made this a particularly fretful period for me was the discovery that I too was included in John's make believe drum kit. But here it was, the start of the drumming career of John 'Bonzo' Bonham!

Though John looked like butter wouldn't melt in his mouth, he had a mischievous bent which came to light during our formative years. It first reared its head when he decided to try riding his tricycle down the stairs of the family home, knocking out his two front teeth in the process. This was followed by deciding (after discovering a tin of orange paint) that one of Jacko's employees would be a much happier man if his motorbike was treated to a new coat of paint. Needless to say, John couldn't understand why he was the only one pleased with the bike's new look. After all, he had truly created a one-off; the only all-orange BSA in Redditch. Maybe all of England.

Previous page
Mick and John Bonham

Above
John Bonham 1948

After his 'impressionist' phase, John returned to hitting everything that didn't move. This time it was with two drum sticks he'd been given as a present. As I was still considered a part of the drum kit I had to keep on the move. Mum assured me that it was just a phase that John was going through and that he'd soon grow out of it, which was all well and good but nobody had explained this to John. He never did grow out of it, but I became pretty nimble on my feet.

The advent of 1953 finally brought me the peace my young self had been yearning for; John started school. This left me feeling safe between the hours of nine and four and I could relax and enjoy my childhood without being one of John's cymbals. Throughout our childhood we were very privileged, some might even say spoilt, thanks to our Grandad's fair sized construction business of which Jacko was a part of. This meant three holidays a year and trips to the different building sites with Jacko. A young boy's dream you might think, but these always caused me more grief because of John's realisation, after watching Jacko hard at work, that things could be hit much harder using a hammer. And thus began John's two future careers – one as a carpenter, the other as one of the loudest drummers in the music business. But of course, all that was a long way off and we were still listening to 78rpm records on the gramophone, and listening to *Children's Favourites* on the wireless. In those days, CD stood for Can Drums.

School was a very large old house in Worcester Road, Redditch called Wilton House Private School and consisted of three classrooms with three lady teachers and a matronly headmistress who, luckily for us, didn't believe in slapping young children if they were naughty. Over the next few years however, that belief would be pushed to the limit by an up and coming drummer and his brother.

By now we'd moved from Hunt End into Redditch, so we were nearer school, which meant a short walk home through the town centre and down Easemore Road, where we lived. At the bottom of our road was another

14

Above
John, Jacko and Mick

school. Given we were walking past this school in our alarming uniforms, taunts like, "Still got yer 'jamas on then," came flying thick and fast. This, of course, was like a red rag to a bull to our John, and out of his mouth would come these fateful words, "Come on our kid, let's get 'em." Now I'm not putting our school down but I don't think they'd taught my dear brother how to count properly.

Either that or there was something wrong with his eyesight, as there was always a gang of them, and only two of us. This, needless to say, was the start of the Hard Fights.

School was way different back then, especially in the discipline department. Not wearing your cap whilst being in uniform would mean a severe lecture (nowadays known as a bollocking). This, I thought, did not apply to me. After all, I was a good boy, my Mum had told me so. That was until that dark and fateful day when, approaching the school gates, I realised I had forgotten my gloves. No big deal, you may be thinking, but on a sliding scale of one to ten in the punishment stakes, this was a two, or even a three. Tears began to flow, the bottom lip began to quiver. Even the backside tensed noticeably. It's at times like this that you realise how much your big brother really does love you, for without hesitation John handed me his gloves and marched into the school yard, hands open to the elements, like Daniel into the lion's den. Boy did he get a bollocking!

After the glove incident I tried very hard to get things right, and all went swimmingly until the day it was reported that some lad had pissed on the toilet floor and the whole school was, somewhat dramatically, called up before the headmistress and the guilty party asked to own up. This time I was on my own. I knew brotherly love would not stretch to rescuing me for something like this. So own up I did, and was made a prefect for my honesty. Now the dictionary definition of 'prefect' is 'school child in position of limited powers over the other pupils'. So I guess the moral of this story is simple – if you can't be 'perfect', be 'prefect'.

The rest of my time at Wilton House passed largely without incident until the day John was ready to go to 'big' school; Lodge Farm Secondary School. By the time I was ready to join him we'd moved back to Hunt End, so it was Ridgeway Comprehensive School for me. I was on my own again.

Above
Mick and John

"I was so keen to play when I left school, I'd have played for nothing. In fact, I did that for a long time, but my parents stuck by me."
– John Bonham

Chapter 2

TIN DRUMS TO TIN PAN ALLEY

John never lost his love for playing the drums throughout his early school years and this was encouraged by a lovely man called Charlie Atkins. The name won't mean much to you, but the music industry owes quite a lot to Charlie Atkins, as it was he who first saw the potential in John Bonham the drummer. He also gave John his first gig.

Now as I mentioned earlier, Jacko had made a few shillings, so we had a caravan and a boat (named *Isobel* after Mum's middle name) down in Stourport-on-Severn, a riverside town about 15 miles from Redditch. We spent most weekends and some of our holidays there, and this is where we met Charlie Atkins. Charlie would spend his weekends in the caravan next to ours, and he was the leader of a dance band. The kind of set-up where the band use Brylcreem and the drummer uses brushes. If you were hip to a tango, waltz or a foxtrot then these were the boys to see. It may not sound exciting now, but to John, this was the business and he would sit and listen to Charlie talk about paradiddles and other such drumming terminology until the cows came home. It was after one of these meetings that Charlie gave John his own set of brushes, which was fine by me because there was no way they would hurt as much as sticks.

By now it had become apparent that this was not a fad John was going through, so he was given a white, pearl snare drum to encourage him in his musical quest. After much practice and more chats with Charlie, John finally got his big break. Charlie asked him to sit in and play drums with the band, at the Caravan Club's Members Dance, and for a kid of 11, this boy "wasn't half bad". There he sat, behind the drums, head full of Brylcreem and brushes in hand giving it his best. This, I believe, was the turning point for John Bonham, and I don't think

'When it came to bullshit,
John could stand with the best
of them.'

that from this point onwards, anyone or anything was ever going to stop him becoming a drummer.

During the years down at the caravan, John and I spent many happy times together. We'd go swimming and, when allowed, take the boat up the river on our own.

Many years later we'd return to the river with John's own boat *Staysea*. Typically John became a dab hand at taking Jacko's boat out on his own without Mum or Jacko knowing, until one lazy Sunday afternoon.

There we were on the boat, having a picnic, when an irate man pulled up alongside in his own boat and started giving Jacko grief about the "laws of the river" and having more respect for other boaters. Jacko, needless to say, was somewhat baffled by the intrusion until the gentleman pointed out that on that very morning *Isobel* had been seen travelling up the river at a rate of knots, causing a wash second only to Moses parting the Red Sea. The effect of this had caused this gentleman to deposit his breakfast all over his nice clean deck. Jacko duly apologised and assured the fellow it would not happen again. Throughout the entire conversation it amazed me how Jacko kept one eye on the irate sailor and one firmly fixed on our John. Yet, somehow John came out with some inspired bullshit and got away with the entire escapade. When it came to bullshit, John could stand with the best of them.

All too soon those days of sun and fun came to an end and it was back to different schools and different friends. Yet whether he was on holiday or with friends, John's mind was never far from drumming. So, during the following months, John saved his pocket money and other monies he had earned, doing odd jobs, and went off looking for items to add to his snare drum and brushes. After a while, he built up a drum kit of sorts, consisting of a snare drum, bass drum and floor tom, all of second-hand origin. He loved it and it would do the trick for now.

Throughout the early 50s, the music scene was being

Above
John Henry Bonham (Jacko)

Above
Joan Bonham

dominated by names like Al Martino, Doris Day, Frankie Lane and Nat King Cole, yet by the end of the decade a distinctive change was starting to take place. It was a change that would take John with it. Until this point, the only real influence of John, bar Charlie Atkins, had been Edmundo Ross and his Band, who, for those that don't know, were one of the best, if not *the* best, Latin American music bands to travel the airwaves. The very pronounced drumming riffs and heavy percussion inspired John even more. We would sit in front of the 'wireless' every Saturday and listen to Edmundo's show, which was a rare treat seeing as there were only three choices of music at home: Jacko's Lena Horne albums, Mum's Frank Sinatra records, and *Children's Favourite* for us kids. Nevertheless, it was all making way for a new era of sound drifting over from America, namely Rock'n'Roll.

Suddenly names like Little Richard, Bill Haley and Elvis Presley were coming to the forefront of popular music and encouraging home-grown artists like Cliff Richard, Marty Wilde, Adam Faith and good old Lonnie Donegan, who John would eventually meet many years after when he was invited to play drums on Lonnie's comeback album.

Until now, the only drummers really heard of were of the Big Band variety. As both Mum and Jacko were big fans (the latter a keen Harry James Band devotee, the former fond of Benny Goodman), John was repeatedly playing a record called 'Don't Be That Way' and 'Swing, Swing, Swing', which featured a drummer called Gene Krupa. John had decided that this was the drummer he wanted to emulate and he spent many hours listening to and learning Krupa's technique. But then it happened. In the penultimate month of the 50s, Sandy Nelson's 'Teen Beat' entered the UK charts and John was mesmerised. So was I, but if you had to sit and listen to it over and over again for three days on the trot while he tried to learn it, you'd be bloody mesmerised as well! It was like kick starting a Harley Davidson – John was off, saying he was going to form a band.

I was going to be involved in this venture too, given the highly honoured title of 'lyricist'. "Lovely job," I thought, but let me tell you that it meant something totally different back then. It meant that I was to be the dipshit that went to the record shop to buy the records and then sit down in front of the stereogram, listen to them repeatedly, and write down the words. A boring job, but I guess someone had to do it, and it was for the good of the band. My first assignment was 'Running Bear' by Johnnie Preston, a nice song but it hardly inspired me. The next record, however, did move me. In fact, I reckon it was one of the best singles ever released – 'Till I Kissed You' by The Everley Brothers.

Apart from the American artists that were changing the mood of music with their influx of Rock'n'Roll, Britain was raising its own fine talent. One of these was Joe Brown. He'd originally formed the Spacemen skiffle group in 1956 and, with a change of direction and name, Joe had his first hit in 1960 with his version of 'Darktown Strutters Ball'. Now under the handle of Joe Brown and the Bruvvers, a string of hits would follow. During this period John and I were holidaying in Brighton, on the South Coast of England, and we managed to get tickets for a Joe Brown show. With our parents' permission, we set off with baited breath. What we saw that night left us quite stunned.

There was Joe Brown, guitar behind his head, playing a solo as he tore into a version of The Spotniks' 1963 hit 'Have Nagila'. I remember saying to John after the show, "Shit, that was good."

It was after this holiday that John returned to school and made friends with another aspiring young musician called John Hill, who played guitar.

Together they decided to form a band, but before they got started they would spend many a night setting up the drum kit, leaning the guitar against it and standing back staring at their mock stage set up – moving it every now and then for better effect. I was never involved in these rituals because I was still sitting in front of the bloody

Above
John (on tour) fourth from left

stereogram, listening to more bloody records and writing down more bloody lyrics! The name of the band would be the 'Avengers' but they unfortunately never got a gig.

Still, time was passing and the day finally arrived when John had to put all his belongings into a satchel and leave Lodge Farm School. This wouldn't leave him too upset; John had never claimed to be an A1 student, always preferring to use his hands, rather than his head. This latter fact was made clear by the headmaster Mr Gordon Antiss, a tall lean man who ruled by the cane. At the final school assembly, whilst addressing the pupils, Mr Antiss said that John would probably not even make a good dustman. Now maybe he was right, but our John wasn't going to hang around to find out – he was already a none too shabby drummer and was set on achieving a much higher accolade.

During his transition from school to work, all John could think about was how to form a band and how he could earn money from playing his drums. At the time, this proved a bit more difficult than he'd have liked, and so he had to revert to Plan B, which was to find a band already doing the round, and in true John Bonham style, muscle in on the act. The best course of action for this was to hang around the Redditch Youth Club, which was about the only place where we could see bands and it was at this establishment that we caught up with The Blue Star Trio. The group comprised of Terry Beale and Mick Ellis, a pair of guitarists and singers who had played together after splitting with The Nighthawks, until someone suggested they might sound better if they had a drummer, so enter Bill Harvey.

The Blue Star Trio played a mixture of pop and ballroom dance music and were becoming quite popular in the area, so much so that they were invited to an audition at the West End Ballroom in Birmingham, to see if they were good enough to play a season at Butlins. Unfortunately for them they narrowly missed getting the gig, and it wasn't long after this that Bill Harvey decided to quit, leaving space for a new drummer. John was in.

Above
John's first newspaper article. Left to right: John Bonham, Terry Beale and Mickey Ellis

As reported in the local paper on 16 July 1963, the Blue Star Trio had been made the resident band at the Redditch Youth Club and every Wednesday night the hall was packed to the rafters with an enthusiastic crowd, who couldn't get enough of Redditch's answer to the burgeoning Liverpool scene. The ensuing write-up was so good that I wanted to go and see them myself, and yes, the hall was filled, but the night I went, it was filled with mums, dads, uncles, aunts and any other family members who could be roped in. And huddled in the corner, were the paying customers.

This sudden fame did not bring untold riches, but something infinitely better; the adoration of young girls. With the era of free love still some way off, your best chances in those days of getting anywhere with the fairer sex was through being either a singer or a musician and, although being sought after by young girls in posh frocks and ankle socks may not quite have been Rock'n'Roll debauchery, it was a start. Over a period of time Mum and Jacko watched John struggle with his endeavours, but realising it wasn't just a fad he was going through, bought him a full set of drums; a sparkling red Trixon set.

Chapter 3

THE LONG AND WINDING ROAD

The 60s kicked off with a musical explosion, the after-effects of which can still be felt some 35 years on. Yet it all seemed to start over-night and suddenly you had groups cropping up all over the place. There must have been at least two groups to every square mile and if a place sold alcohol and had a stage then you could guarantee there'd be a band playing there.

As the music industry developed there was no way John was going to be left behind. Having successfully completed phase one, phase two entailed finding a job. This was a major priority as you couldn't look flash without the cash, but what could he do? He'd never given his future much thought. This is where he made Jacko an offer he simply couldn't refuse; "Let me work for you so I can earn some money and then I won't have to borrow off you anymore." Well I suppose Jacko thought nothing from nothing leaves nothing, so he started him as an apprentice carpenter. John would have to start at the bottom and do all the menial tasks about the building site then train as a carpenter like his father, thus moving slowly up the ladder of success.

It came as a big shock for John to discover there were two seven o'clocks in the day and that he had to be up and ready for the first one. There would be no favouritism towards John simply because he was the gaffer's son. He was to work a full shift, which started at 7.30am and finished at 5.30pm. It wasn't quite as bad as it sounds, as you had a ten-minute tea break in the morning, half an hour for lunch and if you were really lucky, another cup of tea would be brought to where you were working at 3pm, usually served out of a bucket.

John would find this all very hard, because he spent most of the day with his head in the clouds thinking about being in a band. This didn't impress the Foreman, who

"When I left school I went into the trade with my Dad. He had a building business, and I used to like it. But, drumming was the only thing I was any good at, and I stuck at that for three or four years. If things got bad I could always go back to building."
– John Bonham

gave John a lot of grief while he worked for Jacko. He was a powerful looking man, by the name of Eric Twinberrow, and he didn't take any shit. He also had a sense of humour like a kamikaze pilot with piles. Twink, as he was known, kept a close eye on our John, who wasn't appreciated, but he did stick the job out longer than we'd expected. I can imagine that it was on a cold, wet, windy day that saw John sitting there with rain running down his face and his fingers numb from cold that he decided, 'Bollocks this for a game of soldiers' and set off down the road.

This minor set back to John's career didn't get him down because it didn't get him up early either and the quest for a drummer's life was still a dream he wanted to fulfil. He had realised that shops didn't open until 9.00am which was a much more humane time to start work and would suit him much better. After tramping around the Redditch shopping centre for a couple of hours he happened upon George Osbourne & Son, a high class tailors and outfitters who were looking for an assistant. After tidying himself up and five minutes of bullshit, the job was his. He settled in well and the job allowed him to wear the smart suits of the day, which he loved. He'd spend hours in front of the mirror making sure the Windsor knot was just right, his trouser creases would cut paper and it was on with the cuff links and off to work on the bus.

Starting work at 9.00am proved to be much more to John's liking, as it allowed him to play with a band at night and not worry about having to get up at some ludicrous time the next morning. Along with the change of job also came a change of bands. He left the Blue Star Trio and joined up with Terry Webb and the Spiders, who were playing regularly around town. They could also get gigs at the Alcester Trades and Labour Club, where on occasions big named acts appeared.

"When I was 16 I joined my first group. You'll die at the name – Terry Webb and the Spiders. We used to wear purple jackets with velvet lapels. The singer wore a gold lame jacket, and we had greased hair and string ties. It lasted about a year.

Then I joined a group called Way of Life. I got married, most of the others also got married, and it broke up."

What a band wore on stage was sometimes as important as the music they played and the Spiders were no different. They would go on stage wearing sparkling purple jackets with velvet collars and cowboy shoestring ties, while Terry would strut his stuff in a gold lame jacket. As luck would have it they were booked to support Brian Poole and the Tremeloes at the club, which would be a big night. The Tremeloes had already scored two hit singles with a cover of the Isley Brothers 'Twist And Shout' and a song called 'Do you Love Me', which had originally been recorded by The Contours. They were also the band Decca had signed instead of The Beatles. So the Spiders had to be at their best when they took to the stage that night.

They rehearsed a lot, intent that no one would cock up the set and there was a lot of excited talk about this being their big break, but when the night was upon them, they set off for the gig in purple jackets and with frayed nerves. Everyone except for John, that is. Panic set in. All the instruments were there but they had no bloody drummer. Time ticked away and Brian and the Trems had arrived and were busy sorting out where all the gear would be set on the stage. With all the amps, speaker cabinets and microphones set it was noticed that John still hadn't arrived because there was still a pile of drums and cymbals in the middle of the dance floor. Well the shit was ready to hit the fan now because people had started to fill the hall and beer had started to fill tables. Thankfully, Dave Munden, drummer with the Trems, set up John's kit for him, then wouldn't you know it, in walked John with that 'what seems to be the problem?' look on his face. On went his jacket, on went the show, and it was a very good show, but sadly not the break the band was looking for. All I heard about for the next three weeks was how the drummer from The Tremeloes had set his kit up, which really chuffed him to bits.

Chapter 4

BRUM BEAT

Brum was fast becoming a cauldron of new bands and great venues and John knew if he wanted to get on he would have to get into a local band, and quick. The first major problem this new task posed was how to get his drum kit to Birmingham on a regular basis. He couldn't carry it in a bag and onto a bus, so he needed to find a friend with a van. Back then, if you had access to a van then you were laughing, because every band out there needed a roadie. I use the term lightly because a roadie in those days wasn't the bloke who wore a fancy pass around his neck, but a man of steel who would be able to drive all night, unload and load up all the gear, drink like a fish, listen to all the bullshit about when he would get paid and know where the nearest all night fish and chip shop was. One of the greatest exponents of this trade, who we would meet later, was Matthew Stanisewsky, better known as Matt Maloney on account of no one being able to pronounce his surname. Meanwhile, back in Redditch, there were only two people with access to a van. One, a very robust chap who sold hot dogs from the back of his van, when he wasn't working with a band and who went by the apt name of Pumper Phil. The only problem with Phil was that he was already working with a band, Chances Are, formerly known as The Trolls and who featured John's old mate, John Hill. The other was a close friend of John's called Eddie Conoly, who didn't actually have a van, but at least he could drive. Eddie got the job, so all they needed now was a van. Enter Jacko, who had a couple of vans he used for work, so John had a driver, he had a van and he was off to Brum.

John immediately struck lucky meeting up with an old musical colleague, Terry Beale, with whom he had been in the Blue Star Trio and was now appearing regularly with The Senators. It didn't take John long before he too was appearing with The Senators and not long after the band were asked to contribute to an album of local talent, named 'Brum Beat' to be released in 1964 on the Dial label. The band would choose one of Terry's own compositions, an up tempo number entitled 'She's a Mod', which not only allowed John to drum, but also to contribute backing vocals as well. There is a rumour that it was this song that prompted Steven Stills and David Crosby to go with Graham Nash, but I never heard it substantiated. Nevertheless, John was well chuffed that he had made a record, although it would be another five years before he would actually make the charts.

Joining The Senators on 'Brum Beat' were similar local acts like The Crescendos, The Shakes, The Grasshoppers, The Solitaires and The Renegades, and although you may be thinking 'Who?' I have to say that some of the best musicians I have ever seen are still out there, spending hours travelling up and down motorways, cramped into the backs of vans. I still have a copy of 'Brum Beat' and still play it – but why shouldn't I? John made me buy a copy with my own money. 'Brum Beat' may not have been a big seller (catalogue number DLP1 and I don't know if Dial Records ever got to DLP2!), but through it John became better known around the city. And although it wasn't the big break he was looking for, he enjoyed his time with The Senators, even if he always kept an eye out for a better band.

From day one, John and I had always shared a bedroom, even though our house had plenty of rooms. It was just great to be able to natter about the day's events and what tomorrow would bring. Another good reason for sharing was that if we had a fight, and Jeez we had a few, I hadn't got far to fall or something soft to land on.

Most nights he'd tell me stories about Birmingham from behind blurry eyes. The aim of most bands playing in Brum was to get on the 'circuit', the name given to venues owned by the Reagan family. These included The Cavern, Old Hill Plaza, Handworth Plaza and The Ritz in Kings Heath. These were the main places to play, and lesser venues included The Station at

Selly Oak, The Selly Park Tavern, The Black Horse at Northfield, The Bull at Yardley and of course the Whiskey A Go Go in the city centre. There was always somewhere a good band could get a gig, a good drink and a good hiding if you were unlucky. Bands without a definite booking would drive around all the venues in the hope that the booked band didn't show and you got the chance of a gig. Every band without a secured gig drove around the city in Commer 15cwt vans, looking like something out of a Keystone Cops movie. By the time you arrived at the venue you couldn't get anywhere near, because of all the vans that were parked there. It was on a night like this that John and Eddie rolled up at the Old Hill Plaza, not to play but to have a drink and a dance. And it wasn't a band that caught our John's eye, but a young girl he'd end up spending the rest of his life with.

Pat and Beryl Phillips were also on a night out and as they danced, John was watching and building up the nerve to ask for a dance. As they did, John's attention was drawn to Pat, and it was she who he would ask if he could see again. From that night Pat and Beryl would follow John Bonham's career and go to most of his gigs.

Music was changing and so was the appearance of those who made it. Fancy suits and ties were cast aside in favour of bright clothes and a more flamboyant look. Loud clothes to match loud music. The Rolling Stones and The Who were now belting out a kind of music that kicked off a whole new

'John had been so impressed when he saw The Who's drummer, a young Keith Moon, for the first time on TV, that he began to experiment with fashion.'

ball game. Indeed, John had been so impressed when he saw The Who's drummer, a young Keith Moon, for the first time on TV, that he began to experiment with fashion. He had some good ideas too. For his first creation, he had a milkman's white jacket with patch pockets. Firstly, he took the pockets off and dyed the jacket yellow. He then dyed the pockets red, blue and green and then got Mum to sew them back on again. Not only did he have the bottle ('scuse the pun) to design such a garment, but also to wear it on the bus! Next up was more elaborate – a long frock coat he had Mum make him out of some dark green curtain material, with lime flowers all over it. As you can imagine, he was often given a wide berth when waiting for the bus. But not by Harold Bagby, Harold was a smashing chap who lived a little way down the road from our house in Enfield Road and was blind. He would always stand and chat to John as they waited for the bus and although he couldn't see John's bright exterior, he could see deeper and liked what he 'saw'. Harold's dog was a different matter however, and would just whimper quietly.

John's 'piece de resistance' would be an orange suede Levi style jacket with a black leather collar. He immediately dyed the collar green and I immediately fell in love with it. Luckily I managed to buy this jacket when John was stuck for a few readies and he reckoned it was a bargain for five quid, owing to its 'one off' status. Unlike John, I never had the bottle to wear it – all I wanted to do was hang it in my wardrobe happy in the knowledge that I owned such a garment. Or so I thought. Some time later John took me to a party in Dudley and to my surprise another partygoer was wearing an identical jacket. Quizzing the fellow, I enquired after his own jacket, to which he promptly replied that it was, "the only one of its kind and I got it off your kid". Boing!! The fellow in question was Bev Bevan and John had given it to him so he would let him get up and play a few numbers with The Move. The occasion had been John's stag night at The Railway Pub in Kings Heath, where The Move just happened to be playing. Another fond memory of that party was that John had gone mad about a record he had found, 'Stay

'I awoke to see a silhouette of what I thought was Jesus.'

With Me' by Lorraine Ellison. He played it over and over and over again, until everyone had gone home or fallen into an alcohol induced sleep.

John's wanderings around Brum eventually brought him into contact with another aspiring singer by the name of Robert Plant. Robert was a blues man with an unusual but powerful voice, that impressed John so much that he joined up with him in The Crawling King Snakes. Though their first get together didn't last very long, I did get to meet Robert, although it scared the shit out of me. I'd been fast asleep late one night when John had brought Robert back to our house in Hunt End. My bedroom door was open when Robert came upstairs to use the toilet and by mistake came into my bedroom. I awoke to see a silhouette of what I thought was Jesus. With the long curly hair he looked just like the pictures I'd seen at Sunday school and immediately thought 'HE' had come for me. When I promised to stop wetting the bed he went away, but I remember putting the light on and leaving it on until morning.

Things still weren't happening fast enough for John's liking, so he changed bands yet again, this time to Way of Life who featured Reg Jones (vocals), Chrissie Jones (guitar) and Dave Pegg (bass). The latter has since gone on to enjoy a very long musical career with Fairport Convention and is still out there touring to this day. Yet while all this was going on another bunch of local lads were jamming together down at Birmingham's Cedar Club. Ex-Mike Sheridan and the Nightriders guitarist Roy Wood, bassist Chris 'Ace' Kefford, drummer Bev Bevan and vocalist Carl Wayne and second guitarist Trevor Burton, had joined forces to form the aforementioned The Move. Other Brummies were also stamping their name onto the music scene. Ex-Diplomat Denny Laine had formed the Moody Blues with Mike Pinder, Ray Thomas, Graham Edge and Clint Warwick, and had topped the charts with 'Go Now' and The Spencer Davis Group featured one of the most talented vocalists in Steve Winwood. So John went into one of his 'everyone's making it big but me' eras, but undeterred he tried harder and went from band to band in his search

Above
Robert Plant

33

of success, playing with Danny King and the Mayfair Set, Pat Wayne and the Beachcombers and a couple of bands who only lasted a couple of nights, before he hooked up with the Nicky James Movement, a band who had seen the likes of Mike Pinder and Roy Wood pass through their ranks.

One of the band's problems was that their PA equipment was on hire purchase and was often being re-possessed through non-payments. Once, while they were travelling down the motorway, they were forced onto the hard shoulder and had the equipment removed. And on another occasion when they were playing The Station in Selly Oak, two men walked in, unplugged the equipment and took it away while they were mid-concert. It wouldn't have happened to Spinal Tap.

JOHN BONHAM PRE-ZEPPELIN BANDS

The Blue Star Trio

John Bonham played with the Blue Star Trio for a short period in 1963, replacing Bill Harvey on drums.

Terry Beale – guitar and vocals.
Mick(ey) Ellis – guitar and vocals.

The Senators

John played drums with The Senators several times in 1964, plus occasional backing vocals.

The band released a track written by Terry Child called 'She's a Mod' on an LP called 'Brum Beat' which was a successful compilation featuring Birmingham bands.

The Senators had a residency at The Navigation Inn in Coventry.

Band members included Bobby Child vocals and Terry Beale on guitar and vocals.

The young John Bonham played with a number of local groups in 1964/65 including:

Terry Webb and the Spiders

John's first real group, which he joined when he was 16 years old. Noted for their stage clothes, which included purple jackets with velvet lapels and a gold lame jacketed singer.

Pat Wayne and the Beachcombers

John sat in on several occasions. The regular line-up was:

Pat Wayne – vocals
Dario Capaldi – sax.
Mal Edwards – bass
Brian Finch – sax.
Jeff Roberts – lead guitar
Brian Sharpe – drums

The Nicky James Movement

In 1965 John played with The Nicky James Movement. At various times other group members included Roy Wood and Bev Bevan, who went on to form The Move, and Mike Pinder, later to become one of The Moody Blues.

Nicky James also played with Denny Laine and the Diplomats.

Above
The Nicky James Movement
John Bonham second left

Steve Brett and the Mavericks

The group underwent several changes of line-up, and at various times included the Wolverhampton born Dave Holland on bass, who went on to play with Miles Davis. Noddy (Neville) Holder, of Slade fame, featured on guitar and vocals in a later incarnation of the group.

In 1964, around the time that John Bonham played, the members included:

Steve Brett – vocals and guitar
Rick Dene – bass
Gary James – drums
Robert Nelson – lead guitar
Dave Holland – bass

Danny King and the Mayfair Set

With Danny King on vocals, this group included Trevor Burton on guitar until 1966, when he left to become a member of hit makers The Move.

Way of Life

In 1966, aged 17, John joined Way of life, staying for a total of 18 months. He took a break from the band and returned for a short time in 1967.

John sang lead vocals on 'Hey Joe'. See also, the interview with Reg Jones.

Mike Hopkins – lead guitar
Tony Clarkson – bass
John Bonham – drums
Reg Jones – vocals
Chris Jones – guitar (the Jones brothers are uncles to Ace Kefford of The Move)

Later line-ups included Danny King on bass and vocals and then Dave Pegg (of Fairport Convention fame) on bass. See also the interview with Dave Pegg.

The band sometimes featured two drummers: Bonham and Bugsy Eastwood (later to join Dave Pegg and John Hill in The Exceptions).

Way of Life once played support to The Kinks at The Plaza in Handsworth, Birmingham.

The Crawling King Snakes

In 1967 John played with Robert Plant in The Crawling King Snakes, gigging around the West Midlands between his two stints with A Way of Life.

Ian 'Inky' Watts – lead guitar
Bruce 'Maverick' Oakes – bass
Johnny Pasternak – guitar
Nigel Knowles – drums prior to Bonham

Band of Joy

The first Band of Joy was a semi-pro. band, formed in 1966 and notable for the band having painted faces, and a bass player who often dived off the stage into the audience.

A regular early version of the band was Vernon Prarrera on guitar, Robert Plant on vocals, Pete 'Plug' Robinson on drums, Mick Reeves on bass and Chris Brown on organ. Pete Robinson was later to be a member of Bronco.

At various times, Lyddon Laney and John Trickett also played in Band of Joy.

Robert Plant regularly drove the band van to gigs.

Due to musical differences (trad.) Robert Plant was ousted by the manager (actually the father of Chris Brown) and formed a new Band of Joy:

Robert Plant – vocals
Kevyn Gammond – guitar
Paul Lockey – bass
John Bonham – drums

In 1967 when John Trickett left the original band, John Bonham took over the drum seat, and as a pro. band they had regular residencies at the Middle Earth and Marquee clubs in London.

Robert Plant: "In came this fantastic guitarist Kevyn, and we hit it off well. We had a good bass player and John Bonham came in on drums.

It was debatable whether he'd join because it was a long way to go and pick him up, and we didn't know whether we would have the petrol money to get over to Redditch and back! We always laugh about that."

"It turned out to be a really good group. It was a combination of what we wrote ourselves, which wasn't incredible, and re- arrangements of things like 'She Has Funny Cars' and 'Plastic Fantastic Lover'."

A set of recordings were laid down at Regent Sound Studios in London in 1967. Robert Plant donated 'Adriatic Sea View' from this session, to a Kidderminster College fund-raising tape project in 1989, later to be released on CD.

Songs recorded at the session were:
Adriatic Sea View (later released on the MAS Records label);
For What it's Worth (now available on Sixty Six to Timbuktu);
Hey Joe (now available on Sixty-Six to Timbuktu);
Memory Lane.

Opposite
Band of Joy

(Memory Lane was the first song written by Plant and Bonham and is about a street called Dagger Lane in West Bromwich.)

The live set included:
Hey Joe
Sweet Mary
For What it's Worth
If I Were a Carpenter
Hang on to a Dream

Band of Joy averaged £60 – £70 per night for performances.

Kevyn Gammond is currently the joint head of MAS (Mighty Atom Smasher) which is a music project and record label, launched from Kidderminster College in the West Midlands for students of music, with patronage and help from Robert Plant. Kevyn is also the manager of the music management course at the college, active in the local music scene, and renowned for his multi-fret prowess, still resonating from his performances with the Priory of Brion with his close friend Robert Plant.

Paul Lockey is now a teacher and part-time musician.

Robert Plant and John Bonham planned a re-union, a benefit gig for the family of Vernon Prarrera, which did not materialize due to Led Zeppelin commitments and family problems. Some charity gigs did take place in pubs in Kidderminster and Birmingham with Plant, Gammond and Lockey playing in honour of members of a band called Possessed who died in a road accident. Plans to record never came to fruition.

In 1978 Polydor released an LP called 'Band of Joy' recorded in Worcester by a new, five piece line-up featuring Kevyn Gammond and Paul Lockey.

In 1968 a gig supporting Tim Rose led to Bonham being approached by Tim Rose to join his touring band. He accepted.

Band of Joy split up, and Robert Plant worked with, and recorded one track 'Operator' with blues godfather Alexis Korner and pianist Steve Miller.

Kevyn Gammond was born and raised in Kidderminster in the West Midlands, and formed The Shakedown Sound with Jess Roden in 1965. He has known Robert Plant since they were both 17 years old.

The Shakedown Sound were a local success, and supported The Rolling Stones, Walker Bothers and Lulu, sometimes playing up to four gigs a night locally.

They also backed visiting US blues men T. Bone Walker, Buddy Guy, Memphis Slim and Little Walter.

Following a move to London, a mod influence took over, leading to support at The Who and Small Faces concerts.

After the Band of Joy split up, Gammond worked and recorded with Jimmy Cliff, and played on the same bill as Jimi Hendrix in Nottingham.

A European tour with Jimmy Witherspoon, and jamming with the likes of Ben Webster and Art Farmer honed his skills as a guitarist with originality.

Bronco was formed, with Robbie Blunt (later to play in Robert Plants' band), Jess Roden, Pete Robinson, John Pasternak and Kevyn Gammond. Two albums with this line-up were released on the Island label, and a final release after the premature death of John Pasternack on Polydor in 1978.

Tim Rose

John toured in the UK with Tim Rose. He joined the band in June 1968. There are no recordings of Bonzo with Tim Rose.

Tim Rose – Guitar and vocals
Steve Dolan – bass
John Bonham – drums

REG JONES INTERVIEW – 30 OCTOBER 2001

Friend of John Bonham and vocalist with Way of Life.

Q: Well, how did you meet him and how did you get together?

RG: First of all, with Way of Life which is the band that my brother Chris and I played in. We were holding auditions on a Sunday afternoon at The Cedar Club in Birmingham and we had about 20 drummers turn up for this audition, John came along and said, "What gigs we got then?" and I thought blimey he's cocky, you know, what gigs we got, even before he'd had his audition! I said well you seem pretty confident, anyway he got the job and we did a gig on the same night at The Cedar Club.

Q: You played that night?!

RG: Yeah, we were already set up you see because we'd been booked to play there and he'd passed his audition of course. We were doing Motown and Progressive Rock which was popular at the time, quite a variation with some of our own original numbers as well. At the end of the night, about 2am in the morning, I had a disagreement with John because he wanted me to take some girls home for him in the van and I told him that I'm not running groupies around for you in the middle of the night and if you are going to be this cocky after the first gig, then it might as well be your last, so I sacked him on the first night. The next morning we were rehearsing, well it was about 12o'clock actually 'cos musicians have trouble getting up in the morning. My brother Chris and Mike 'Sprikey' Hopkins, who I think went on to play with The Quartz, were both on lead guitar and Tony Clarkson was on bass, who was in the 'World of Oz'. We were getting the gear out of the van ready to rehearse and who should be stood watching us, wearing what I used to call his 'Harold Wilson' pinstripe suit carrying a little suitcase, but John. I felt sorry for him, so I said look if you're gonna be in my band, what I say goes, he said okay, he was back in the band and rehearsed with us that afternoon.

Q: Was that the original line-up?

RG: That was the original line-up, we wanted to spend time rehearsing before we started the gig. We hadn't got much money and it was difficult for me to pick everyone up from all over Birmingham in the van each time. It was summer, so I came up with the idea of hiring a caravan in Great Yarmouth for a couple of weeks for us all to rehearse in. On the way to Great Yarmouth I soon realised that not one of us had got any money, not such a good idea after all, we barely rehearsed and I ended up paying for everything.

Q: Was this before Dave Pegg joined?

RG: Yes, Danny King played bass before Peggy joined us, this was after Tony and Sprikey had left.

Danny was a great singer as well, we played a big venue in Loughborough and there was an eleven piece soul band on before us, they were all wearing red shirts which they ripped off on the last number, they were really giving it some! Then the four of us came on stage and the whole audience rushed to the front to watch our set, they had an eleven piece band on and it was though they hadn't even noticed them. Chris, John and I were half way through our number when I spotted Danny King down in the audience, still playing his bass. I said, "What are you doing down there?" He said, "It's such a powerful sound, I wanted to be on the receiving end of it!"

It was soon after that, that we did a double gig, we played Parkinson Cowan on the evening and the Elbow Room later on that night, we had Danny King with us on the early gig and Dave Pegg at the Elbow Room. We had two separate bass players on the same night which was quite unheard of in those days. That's when Dave first joined the band.

Q: Any funny stories from those days?

RG: Oh, yeah, John was always up to something, he and I were best mates for years, he actually lived at my mum's house for a while. We used to go out drinking in Warstock and Kings Heath. I remember when he tried to grow a moustache. He was only young of course then. We played at Norwich Industrial Club and to look more mature, he had thickened his moustache up with mascara, he was standing at the bar chatting to some girls saying, "Looks pretty good doesn't it?" and all of a sudden from the heat of the lights and sweat from playing, his moustache started to run down his face, he didn't know it was, but the rest of the band had a good laugh about it.

Q: This would be around 1966/67 wouldn't it?

RG: Yeah, we were set up to play a gig at The Ritz, Kings Heath and the World Cup was on television before the gig. Old man Reagan, the gaffer, said if anybody can come and do a commentary on the match, the winner would get a bottle. John volunteered himself and dragged me with him onto the stage, he stood at the microphone, went "Errrr…" And left it to me.

Q: He left you to it?

RG: Yeah and I won. Actually the prize was a bottle of whiskey, I remember because we went down to The Cedar Club after the gig and he drank it!

Q: What do you think influenced John's style?

RG: I know where he got his influences from, because he told me. He used to cross Rock'n'Roll beats with soul rhythms, he liked the Isley Brothers drumming rhythms and he'd cross the two styles together to get his unique sound. Perhaps that's how he got such a powerful sound, his triplets on the bass drum were just superb. He was so loud we never used to mike up his drum kit at gigs and still constantly got complaints about the volume.

Q: I heard that John used to sing?

RG: Yes, John used to sing the lead on 'Hey Joe' and we used to do the backing vocals.

Q: Matthew was your roadie at this time wasn't he, with a Commer van?

RG: John had just started playing with the band. I had a yellow Commer and one night we were on our way to The Cedar Club and it broke down, so John phoned his mate, Matthew, and Matthew came to rescue us in his green Commer. From that day on he became the roadie. We weren't a professional band in those days, but there were always plenty of gigs.

RG: Can you remember what you were earning, like £10, £20?

A: Yes, it wasn't much, we used to blow it on a curry, it didn't seem to matter then and anyway we were all single. I used to collect the wages and pay the band, but we always gave poor Matthew the excuse that we had been paid by cheque and couldn't pay him. One night he collected the wages before I could, to stop us from taking it off him. After the gig, Big Al, the gaffer at the Rum Runner said, "You'd better have a look at your roadie." And there he was pissed out of his brains lying on the floor, he'd spent all our wages on booze and drank the lot whilst we were on stage.

Q: So you used to enjoy yourselves?

RG: We were playing at The Plaza, Handsworth and we were going to have a party after the gig, so we decided to borrow some glasses from the club. Matthew filled John's bass drum case full of empty beer glasses, but on his way out of the club he managed to drop the drum case from the top of the stairs, the gaffer, Alan Reagan, was stood at the boot and all of these glasses fell out at his feet. But he was a nice bloke and said, "Have a good party, you're playing here on Monday, so bring as many back as you can."

Q: There were times when you played on the same bill as Slade, The Move and other local bands?

RG: We played a Flower Power party in a marquee in Balsall Heath with The Move, Ace Kefford from The Move is my nephew. That's when John took these big plastic flowers and covered his whole kit in them. The audience couldn't believe it, this big powerful sound coming from behind a mass of flowers.

Q: How long was John with you?

RG: John was with us for about 18 months. He was very extrovert and a real play-up merchant, but always serious about his music. He used to play the band up, one night we were coming home from a gig in the van and John started writing these words on the back of a beer mat, he said "It's coming to me, it's started to flow…" as if lyrics to songs just came to him, he really had the bass player on when he wrote down all of the lyrics to The Kinks' number 'Waterloo Sunset', the bass player thought he was a genius and got all excited about this song. We used to rehearse at a recording studio in Birmingham, all John had was his bus fare, so Chris and I would buy him dinner. We would all chip in together. He travelled on the bus because he drove like a maniac, whenever he borrowed his Dad's van, he would do handbrake skids on the gravel.

Q: Dave Pegg mentioned that you were not asked to return to some places because John played too loud.

RG: Well he was loud, we did the 'Tyburn House' one night and the gaffer was really moaning, the gaffers always used to moan, but the audience never did. I got sick of it and I shouted down the mike, "Do you think we're playing too loud?" And they shouted, "No! No!" John got annoyed and threw his cymbal; it hit the wall and stuck in the brick. I used to say that when John struck up, the barmaid's knickers hit the optics! He used to do it deliberately, as soon as I bent down to plug a mike in or something, he would whack his snare and send me deaf.

RG: He didn't have his drums miked up either?

A: No, there was never any need, he had a blue Ludwig Kit that was really loud anyway. It seemed as if he'd get hold of his drum sticks and just attack the drums, but he was totally in control and a solid player.

Q: How do you remember John?

RG: He was a good drummer, when he was young he was one of the nicest people you could have met and we were really good mates. We kept in touch throughout the rest of his life, I remember when Way of Life got a deal with Polydor Records and we were recording at their studios in about 1970. John, Robert Plant and Matthew came to the studio to see how we were doing and wish us luck. We remained friends until the end.

DAVE PEGG INTERVIEW 27 OCTOBER 2001

Bass player with Way of Life, later to be a regular member of Fairport Convention.

Q: You have said, you had heard about John before, but when did you meet him?

DP: I met John when I joined Way of Life with Reggie and Chris Jones. He was living in Redditch at the time in a caravan at his parents' place. I had this purple painted Renault van I bought off Chris' dad Percy and it wouldn't have a problem going anywhere except to Redditch. Whenever it went to Redditch the bonnet would lift up. John didn't drive then, and I used to drive him home after the gigs. There was a hill on the way back to Redditch, and every time we went down it the bonnet would fly up. The first time it happened I thought shit, the lights have gone. I drove him home most nights, and most nights very happy, but probably over the limit.

Q: You had a lot of gear, did you get it all in that Renault?

DP: It was a struggle, but John later got Matt to be roadie and he would drive. At the end of the night we'd get our money (our £15) and Matt would get his share, £3. Then we'd siphon off some petrol to get to the next gig as nobody wanted to part with his cash.

Q: It was reported that John always wanted to push his drums to the front to get noticed. Was that before or after Way Of Life?

DP: I only ever played with John in Way Of Life and he never had to push his drums to the front, because he was so fucking loud the way he played them. It was the loudest drum kit in the world, it was unbelievable. It was the way he tuned the kit, no one else could actually do that to get that bass drum sound, it was phenomenal, you've heard it on all the records, a classic drum sound. We only played about 20 gigs, everywhere we could in the Midlands, most of the time we only played the first half because the promoter would tell us we were too loud and would have to go.

Q: You only played 20 gigs?

DP: About 20 altogether and I remember John and me going to collect the money after the tour, from the agents [Carlton John's] in Wake Green Road. These were the people who run Mother's Club at the time and we got nothing. Mother's was the place to play, Johnny Haynes ran the place, a nice guy who went on to have a great studio, but at that time it was very primitive. Johnny told Bonzo he was unrecordable and should go back to hod carrying for a living. The problem was that he was just too loud, and the equipment he'd got could not cope with the bass drum input level on his mixing desk. When John hit the bass drum it was like the heavens had opened.

Opposite
Dave Pegg and John Bonham

Q: So why did you break up in the end, was it the lack of venues to play?

DP: We broke up because nobody would book us, as we were too loud. There were some classic examples, like the Top Spot in Ross-On-Wye, they had a traffic light system on stage. Bands used to carry their own PA but only for their vocals, you never amplified the guitars or drums through it. Bonzo only hit his bass drum once, and it immediately went too red, turning the power off. This was before we'd played a number.

Q: When you did split up did you keep in touch with Bonzo?

DP: I became a big Zeppelin fan. I joined Fairport Convention, and John and the guys would come and see us as they were quite into the folksy type thing. Sandy sang on their fourth album (Battle of Evermore). We went to see Zeppelin at the Locarno, Coventry when there was a bomb scare, everyone left the building except Robert, who was saying, "What's the matter with you all?" They were a great band, and I was pleased John had got a proper job. I remember visiting him at his flat in Dudley, and he was always renovating it. One time it had got oak panelling and gold bathroom fittings, it was like walking around Rackhams. Outside there were his cars parked, and one time his neighbours complained about his Bentley parked there. We lived at Sutton Coldfield at the time with my mum, and remember him coming round in an old Ford Anglia Estate. He gave me a copy of their first Zeppelin album, which I played on my old Dansette (before the days of stereo) and it sounded absolutely fantastic. Then it was come on, we're off to Welwyn Garden City to see the band. What a great night that was. The next gig I went to see John, he had got a gold Jaguar and Robert had got one too. I thought, what fantastic cars and both were complaining about a bit of noise coming from somewhere. The cars I was used to driving were all noisy.

Q: Knebworth 4 August 1979

DP: Fairport were the opening act and the only act to get paid. We actually got paid for it, which was quite amazing really. Yes Zeppelin got paid but there were a lot of others who didn't get paid. It was quite scary for us as the opening act, and we were supposed to play for an hour. We decided to play all our up-tempo stuff (we were shitting ourselves) it was a sea of painted faces out there waiting for Zeppelin to go on. After 45 mins we ran out of numbers and Tommy Vance shouted over, "Hey, they're really liking this, can you do another half an hour?" So we just played them all again, and got away with it 'cause we got paid.

Q: How would you like to sum up the times spent with John?

DP: Well, he was one of my mates. I have happy memories of John and I never had bad times with him at all. We were good buddies, we had great, great times, and he's sorely missed. He was never shy of buying a round of drinks, even when he had no money, and would always take his turn to siphon petrol, in fact it was him who taught me how to do it, but the first one he showed me, was diesel.

CHRIS JONES INTERVIEW 6 JANUARY 2002

Guitarist with Way of Life, and brother of Reg Jones.

Q: When did you first meet John?

CJ: The first time I saw him was with a young band when he was about 15 years old. The next time was when he came for an audition at the Cedar Club, Birmingham. He was successful and played that night.

Q: I heard that he became close to you, Reg and the family.

CJ: John lived at our house on and off for about two years, and was one of the family, becoming very close to my father. John had a suitcase of clothes he used to carry around to different gigs, but one day he lost it. Dad spoke with him and gave him a wad of cash to get some more. Dad and John were very close, and when Dad died John took the news very badly.

Q: What memories have you got of those early years, with Way of Life? I'd heard he could be eccentric at times.

CJ: Oh yes, he would have some strange ideas. The one gig he turned up with fur all round his drums, boasting to us that they were unique and no one would have drums like these. Problem was it turned out to be his mother's genuine mink coat, which was her pride and joy.

During his time with us we also did a few gigs with two drummers. The guy was Bugsy Eastwood, who later played with Dave Pegg and John Hill in The Exceptions. John and Bugsy would set up at the front of the stage, they got on very well together and we supported The Kinks at the Plaza, Handsworth.

Q: Dave Pegg told me the story about the speakers you and John made, with the help of Jacko's [John's dad] account at the builders merchants.

CJ: John and I built these 4 x 12 speaker cabinets, there were four of them, we built them out of marine ply and covered them with orange vinyl. John's mate, an upholsterer, got the vinyl, and the other materials we put on Jacko's account. They were sensational and we struggled to get them on some of the stages with the rest of the gear. Two of them have stood the test of time, and I still have them in my garage.

Q: John always liked to join in vocally in the early days, what do you remember?

CJ: People underestimated the vocal talent of Way of Life in those days. Several times we would have four part harmonies, Danny King had a great voice, and we had a great sound.

Q: When was the last time you saw John?

CJ: The last time I saw John was when he came to The Bromsgrove Baths, two months before he died. We had got a band together called Prima Donna, with a guy called Sean on the drums and Ace Kefford and myself. We invited John on stage and he played with us. That was the last time.

Chapter 5

NO BLOODY DRUM STICKS

Nicky James 7 May 1991

There are many nights I could tell you about but one in particular comes to mind. John had already been in trouble with his Mum and Dad many times because he kept crashing Jacko's van. So on this particular night he phoned me and said:

"Nicky, you've got to help me."
"Why?" I said.
"Because my Dad won't let me have my drums."
"Why?"
"Because I've pronged the van again."
"You idiot," I said.
"Don't call me an idiot or I'll smack you."

Bless him, he used to smack me regular and we would end up scrapping on the floor. Then we would burst out laughing and go and do the gig. And you know what? It was always a better gig. I promise you, it was a fun thing. Anyway, John said, "Me Dad's locked the drums in the garden shed."

"Can't you get the key?" I asked.
"No, because if I go into the house he'll know what I'm up to and hide the keys or keep them in his pocket."

So we devised a little plan. We had this black and maroon Bedford van with side-loading doors, so I pulled up outside the alleyway that led to the garden and met John round the corner. He popped out from behind a tree and we went round to the shed. We clambered up the wall at the side of the shed then I had to lift the roof up just enough so that John could climb inside and pass the drums out of the window. Everything was going to plan until I accidentally stood on the shed and the bottom end started collapsing. We both fell into the shed, landing amongst his drums, covered in dirt and dust. As we

"I had a group with Nicky James, an incredible lead singer. But we had so much of the equipment on hire-purchase, we'd get stopped at night on the way back from a gig and they'd take back all of the PA"
– John Bonham

scrambled to get out the noise was awful. I was first out, scratched up, clothes ripped and generally covered in shit. John was yelling, "Quick! Grab this," and started passing the gear to me. He was one of the lucky ones in those days because he had drum cases. His Mum and Dad looked after him well, they idolised the bugger. Anyway, he passed out as much as he could before the lights inevitably came on and someone shouted, "Who's that? Is that you John?"

We went running down the alley, banging against the fence and wall, and as we were piling everything into the van we heard a cry of, "Call the police", so we shot off down the road roaring with laughter at what had happened. When we arrived at the gig, I think it was the Adelphi Ballroom in West Bromwich; John began to unpack his kit, only to find he'd left most of it behind. All he had was a snare drum and stand, a bass drum and pedal but no cymbals, no hi-hat and worst of all, no bloody drumsticks. We were the only band playing so we couldn't borrow any off another drummer and that's when I told him he'd have to play with his hands. I'd seen him do it a couple of times before and had asked him if it hurt. "No", he'd replied. "Actually, when I do this it goes down a storm." Well this night he'd have to prove it and that is when he started bashing the drum kit with his hands, he played the whole gig just using his hands and fingers and it was the most exciting gig we ever played. The crowd absolutely loved him.

As far as I'm concerned, John Bonham was a true, total showman. We were just a couple of mates having fun and enjoying what we did. We did have the odd scrap too. I remember one night and someone picked on John. I've never seen anything like it. He went bananas and within seconds he'd turned round and wiped the floor with the bloke. Then he came back to the stage with a huge grin and said, "That weren't too bad were it?"

He could be unpredictable though, and after a while, with the Denny Laines and Mike Pinders, the band movement was starting to happen. They were moving away from solo singers with backing bands and the musicians were starting to sing for themselves. So

'We were the only band playing so we couldn't borrow any off another drummer and that's when I told him he'd have to play with his hands.'

basically I was blown out of the Brum Scene because I was a lead singer of the old style. John went on to do other things.

Looking back, the great thing about the times we had together was that, if we turned up at someone else's gig, the drummer nearly always asked John to get up and play a few numbers and I would get up and sing. John would play anywhere with anybody. He just loved to play. He lived for gigging and, as history proves, he was to become one of the most successful drummers, if not the most successful rock drummer. There are drummers of outstanding ability out there, but John was the first, the man who did it for everyone. It was more than just talent; there was something spiritual about it, because when music and a musician reaches kids 20 to 30 years later, like John does, it really is something special, like The Beatles. They are targets for aspiring musicians. John was one of those drummers. He set a standard, like Gene Krupa did. He's amongst the greats.

Chapter 6

BRUM BEAT II

"I swore to Pat that I'd give up drumming when we got married, but every night I'd come home and just sit down at the drums. I'd be miserable if I didn't."
– John Bonham

After John split with Nicky James he played with several bands, including Steve Brett and the Mavericks and Pat Wayne and the Beachcombers, but, alas, to no avail. That big break he was looking for still eluded him. Yet whilst his musical career seemed to be at a standstill, his love life was blossoming and he married Pat Phillips on February 19, 1966.

During the next couple of years, whilst the pair hunted for their own home, they spent time living at Pat's parents' house on the Priory Estate in Dudley and then our house in Hunt End. After a while they moved into the caravan at the back of the house so they could have some privacy as they raised their baby son, Jason. With a young family to support, John had to turn his hand to finding a proper job and had stints back on the building site for Jacko and also at a wire cordage factory, before ending up at the AEI factory in Birmingham. This latter job he landed thanks to Matt Maloney. Mathew was one of the lucky few that had a van and had been a roadie for his brother Stefan's band when he met up with John. It wasn't long before he started working with him; a position he would keep forever.

1967 was a year when music splintered in many different directions. There were the mods zooming about on their Lambretta and Vespa scooters, listening to The Who and the Small Faces but dancing the night away to Northern Soul music at venues like the Twisted Wheel in Manchester and the Surf Side Stop in Brum, being chased around by big strong hairy blokes on bigger, stronger motorbikes trying to kick their arses. Jimi Hendrix and Cream, featuring Eric Clapton, Ginger Baker and Jack Bruce were becoming the biggest names in music, while across the Atlantic the West Coast sound was attracting a large audience with acts like Jefferson Airplane and Love, with their brilliant 'Forever Changes' album.

'We watched in awe as he played his guitar behind his head, with his teeth, between his legs, lying on the floor and then setting fire to it and smashing it!'

Right
Jimi Hendrix

Back in the venues around Brum, Robert Plant had moved from his blues roots and had become an avid fan of the West Coast sound, which persuaded him to form The Band Of Joy and eventually, after two different line-ups, John would join Robert in the third and final line-up. While John had chosen the West Coast sound, I was back at home with backcombed hair and a Lambretta SX150 scooter, getting ready to tour the country getting my arse kicked.

On a brighter note, while John and Pat lived in the caravan I would spend many nights sitting up with Pat waiting for John to get back from a gig, and it was during this time that I was to meet and become close friends with Beryl, Pat's sister, and Ros Beresford, a bubbly blonde haired girl who was so much fun to be with. On 27 May, after a gig at the Black Horse in Northfield, everybody had gone back to Ros' house for an all night party. You know, the one where the bloke had my orange jacket on! Leaving there at 10.30am the following morning, I met up with the lads and then in a convoy of 12 scooters, we set off on what was to be one of the first major rock concerts. Early on the morning of 29 May we rode into the picturesque market town of Spalding in Lincolnshire. Set in the heart of the bulb growing fields of Eastern England, we were met by the sight of thousands of people congregating outside one of the vast bulb auction halls. The crowd was made up mainly of mods, with a sprinkling of rockers. For one night that small country town became a boiling cauldron of loud music. Geno Washington and the Ram Jam Band warmed up the audience, followed by Brum's own The Move, through to the power of Cream, culminating with the Jimi Hendrix Experience, an act that simply could not be followed.

We watched in awe as he played his guitar behind his head, with his teeth, between his legs, lying on the floor and then setting fire to it and smashing it! Then, as he walked off stage he pushed all the speaker cabs over and disappeared off the stage. I had never witnessed anything like it because, until now the only major gig I'd seen was when my Mum took me to see The Beatles in 1964.

After a good night's sleep in the local bus shelter it was back home to relay what I had seen to John.

Other notable dates of that year were 9 June where, whilst performing at the Cofton Club, John was reprimanded by the manager for playing too loud. John's response? "Loud! I'll show you loud. You won't need to pull another beer, it will just flow out of the taps with the vibration!" Another venue crossed off the gig list! Then, on the 17th he played at Handsworth Plaza as support to The Kinks. But to me the funniest gig was when The Band of Joy played Queen Mary Ballroom in Dudley. One of the cover versions they played was Tim Hardin's 'If I Were a Carpenter'. But unlike the original, their version built up steadily into a powerful crescendo, and it was during the final few bars of the song, as Robert sang out "Marry me, Marry me" he wrapped his legs round one of the pillars at the side of the stage and emulated, what to all intents and purposes, was a knee trembler. That was the final straw for Mum, who had been watching the show. With her handbag hanging from her arm she approached the stage and above the applause you could hear, "John! You get off those drums right now! You're not playing with that boy, he's a pervert!" Not long after this incident The Band of Joy toured the north of England and Scotland, this time John was playing alongside his old mate John Hill, who had joined the band for the tour.

Before he went, John told Pat that if things didn't get better with this tour he would sell his drums and take up a proper job again. Things did not get better, so John returned home and began cleaning his kit in preparation to sell it.

Chapter 7

THROUGH ROSE COLOURED GLASSES

"It really started to happen when I was with Tim Rose. I was doing OK and I was getting offers. Joe Cocker was interested, so was Chris Farlowe and Robert and Jimmy. It was baffling. I had to consider so much. It wasn't just a question of who had the best prospects, but which was going to do the right kind of stuff."
– John Bonham
(interviewed in 1973)

Unknown to John, as he sat despondently cleaning his drums, certain people were scouring the area trying to find him. Although he thought that the last tour had brought no success, little did he know that he'd been spotted supporting an American artist in a ballroom in Nelson, Lancashire.

The artist in question was Tim Rose, who was enjoying much critical acclaim with two hit singles and a big selling album. The first single was 'Hey Joe', released in 1966, a slow moody tune which would later inspire a Jimi Hendrix classic. The second was, for me, the single that really stood out from other records of the time. 'Morning Dew', written by Rose and Bonnie Dobson, became a classic in its own right. Tim's professional career had started in the early 60s, playing guitar with The Journeymen, alongside John Phillips and Scott McKenzie before moving on to join Cass Elliott and James Hendricks in The Big Three. Tim forged his solo career when they split in 1964.

Over the years there have been many accounts on how John had joined up with Tim, so I needed to find out the true story. My only problem was that I hadn't seen Tim for nearly thirty years and hadn't a clue where to look, that was until I was doing some research for the book in my sister Debbie's office/studio in London. Someone using the studio said Tim was living in London and could find out his telephone number and within the hour I had the number. With trepidation I dialed the number, but all my fears disappeared when Tim answered the phone. His enthusiasm for this book overwhelmed me and I felt really chuffed.

While we chatted, he explained that he was to be presented with a special guitar the next day, at a well

known guitar shop in Denmark Street in the West End, called 'Hank's Guitars' and would I like to join him for a chat and a glass of wine.

As soon as it was known I was off to a guitar shop, I was to be accompanied by a very good friend of mine, Pete 'Guitar' Bullick. Pete was my sister Debbie's guitarist and Fiancé and they had just started recording Debbie's album 'The Old Hyde' so he was up for looking at some new guitars. The shop was heaving when we arrived, so after a couple of glasses of wine it was decided that we would meet in a café in Dean Street the following day at 3.00pm.

The next day I met Tim in the café as agreed, and what follows is Tim's recollection of his tour with our John.

Tim Rose

"I had been using a very fine drummer by the name of Aynsley Dunbar, who had learnt his trade with The Mojos, Jeff Beck and John Mayall's Bluesbreakers, when I toured the UK prior to meeting John. Aynsley was unavailable for the 1968 tour, but I remembered seeing a drummer playing with Band Of Joy and thinking 'I want him'. I eventually found John and offered him the job, paying about £40 per week."

I remember John thinking it was the break he had been waiting for, because back then, one pound would get you about eight beers, a bag of chips and you'd still have enough for the bus fare home. For a young married man with a wife and child to support, this was big money.

The line-up for Tim's band featured Steve Dolan on bass, John on drums and Tim on guitar and vocals. With only a short while before the tour was due to start, the band got down to the business of rehearsing. Tim recalls that John's drumming reminded him of Mitch Mitchell from Jimi Hendrix's band. John attempted to impress his new paymaster with additional fancy fills, but Tim told him, "Don't worry John, you've already got the job. Just keep it straight and powerful." Once the set was up to scratch the tour started in June 1968 and the set drew some good reviews. Tony Wilson of the *Melody Maker*, reported:

"If anyone comes close to the rather vague definition 'Folk Rock' it must be Tim Rose. Powerful singing backed by his own electric, augmented by bass and drums on folk based numbers such as 'Morning Dew', 'Long Time Man' and 'Hey Joe' provided a stirring session at Blaises in London last Sunday. These heavy, soulful numbers were balanced by lighter songs such as 'Hello Sunshine' and a five string banjo number 'Foggy Mountain Breakdown' which gave a chance for drummer John Bonham and bass guitarist Steve Dolan to take solos."

With Tim welding the whole thing together with some witty introductions, this was a good evening's entertainment that had guts and excitement, musically.

The tour was well underway and causing quite a buzz around the music business, and by the time the band played London's Marquee club, another aspiring drummer was waiting to see the show. His band was called Hard Meat, and had been booked as support to Tim Rose. As he will tell in his own words later on, he was simply dumbstruck by Rose's drummer, within the first few minutes of the band taking to the stage. Little did he know that some 20 years later he would take John's seat behind Messrs, Page, Plant and Jones, at the 1985 Live Aid concert. Mind you, he didn't do too badly with his own career during those 20 years.

Phil Collins

"I went down to the Marquee club and patiently queued up to get in," Phil recalls. "It was quite new then to do one set instead of two, so I waited until about 10pm when the group came on stage. Within the first few minutes I was dumbstruck by the drummer. He was doing things with his bass drum that I'd never seen or heard before – the last two beats of a triplet, something I've stolen and do whenever possible. He then played a

Opposite
The Yardbirds
(Jimmy Page centre)

62

solo and again I'd never heard or seen a drummer play like that. He played with his hands on the drums – I later found out that as a bricklayer he had very hard hands and it was obvious from seeing him solo that night. I vowed to keep an eye on this guy Bonham and I followed his progress. He was, even then, a major influence on my playing.

"Running a parallel course with this was another favourite band of mine, The Yardbirds. I'd seen Jeff Beck's first gig with them (he'd joined that afternoon) and I'd bought the 'Five Live Yardbirds' album. I'd seen Jimmy Page playing bass after he'd joined in an afternoon and Beck was still on lead guitar. Suddenly they split and the news came of a New Yardbirds. This was something that I had to check out so I went to the Marquee to see them; me and about 50 other people. There they were, absolutely electric. Plant, Page, Jones and Bonham, my heroes. That gig, amongst their first half dozen, was incredible.

"I only came close to meeting John once, at a Melody Maker Awards bash. I was there representing Genesis and Brand X and he, with the rest of the band was picking up their awards.

"Stories of the dark side of Zeppelin are like Phil Seaman stories, everybody has one! They certainly had attitude when they entered a room. All I know is that he was an incredible drummer and I was shocked when I heard of his death. Funnily enough Genesis was at Headley Grange where Zeppelin had recorded some of 'Physical Graffiti' and those legendary drums of 'When The Levee Breaks' from Zep IV recorded on the stairwell.

"A few years passed, when suddenly I received a call from Robert Plant inviting me to play on his first solo album. Here I was, filling a hole left by one of my heroes. I said 'yes' of course. I received a cassette of the material and was amazed by the sound and feel of the drummer on the tape, it turned out to be Jason, John's son. He sounded just like his old man. I came to know and like Jason a lot, we met occasionally and I think he was a bit of a fan of my playing. I felt like taking him under my wing for a while but he did very well without me!

"I completed two albums and his first solo tour with Robert, trying to make him smile the way I knew John did with his playing. Finally at Live Aid in 1985.

"John's boots were just too big for anyone to fill though. He was unique."

John Bonham

While all this was going on, somewhere in another part of London, Jimmy Page and Peter Grant were in discussion about which new musicians they could recruit to form the New Yardbirds. The first new recruit would be John Paul Jones, a highly regarded bass player with whom Jimmy had worked during his early session days. Terry Reid had been short listed for vocals but was unable to join due to other commitments, but he in turn put forward the name of Robert Plant.

Peter and Jimmy went off to take a look at this Black Country boy, who Reid insisted could really belt out a song, and they soon found out they hadn't been misled. Robert was asked to join them in London to discuss his likes and dislikes in music. Robert asked who the drummer was going to be and was told that BJ Wilson had been asked but had declined the offer. Robert remembered his old mate and told them about John, who was touring the country with Tim Rose.

"I had so much to consider before I joined Led Zeppelin. It wasn't a question of who had the best prospects, but which was going to do the right kind of stuff. I knew Joe Cocker was going to make it. But, I already knew from playing in Band of Joy with Robert Plant what he liked, and I knew what Jimmy Page was into, so I decided I liked that sort of music better. And it paid off."

By the time the Rose show had rolled on to the Hampstead Country Club in London, Robert, Jimmy and Peter were there to see the show and find out if this drummer was as good as Robert had claimed. In the end they went to see John on several occasions, as Tim recalls, "They didn't say a lot to me but spent a long time talking to John." It didn't take too long before Tim put two and two together and realised that these infiltrators were out to steal his drummer and was worried enough to confront John, asking, "Are you going to leave me to go with them?" "No way," was the reply he got. "Not only do I love this life, but the money's too good."

I only managed to see the Tim Rose trio once on this tour because I didn't know our kid was going to leave. As I found out, whilst writing this book, neither did Tim. The venue I caught them at was The Wharf Hotel, a riverside pub on the banks of The River Severn at Holt Fleet in Worcestershire. It holds bittersweet memories, as I remember standing at the bar moaning to a bloke next to me about how late it was and the band hadn't even gone on yet. No sooner had the words, "Who is this Tim Rose bloke anyway?" left my mouth than our John and Steve took the stage, along with the chap next to me. I had to miss the first couple of numbers while I took my foot out of my mouth. It wasn't the first time I'd cocked up and it certainly wouldn't be the last, but while I stood watching the band on stage I understood what Tony Wilson from the *Melody Maker* was talking about.

The tour carried on to Middlesborough, and it wasn't until the band actually got there that they realised that John hadn't. Luckily for Tim, Steve was aware of what was going on with their drummer and had another chap ready to fill in. Our John was in Scandinavia with the New Yardbirds.

As we sat in the café sipping our drinks, with Tim telling the story and me listening intently, I noticed a large grin slowly appear on Tim's face as he said, "It was bad enough John doing a runner during the tour but I always wore tinted glasses that John really liked and they did a runner at the same time."

It would be several years before Tim would meet up with

John again but they finally bumped into each other in a hotel in America and the first thing John said was, "Hey Tim, it wasn't me who had your glasses." "But John," Tim replied, "No one knows about the glasses!"

As we parted that afternoon Tim turned to me and said, "You know the sad part about it was we never managed to record anything together." Leaving the café and wandering back to the office I was confused about one thing Tim said. "When John started with me his timing was a bit erratic. His 4/4 timing could vary between 3 and 3/4 and 4 and 1/4." So did John have a problem with his timing? There was only one way to find out and only one person to ask who would know the answer – John Paul Jones.

Above
John Paul Jones

Chapter 8

THE TRAIN STARTS A ROLLING

John Paul Jones

John Paul Jones had formed such a great bond with Bonzo, that it allowed these two great musicians to become a rhythm section that would let Jimmy Page and Robert Plant steer the vehicle in any musical direction only to find, upon their return, that the beat was still rock solid. They would perform solos too; Bonzo with 'Moby Dick' and Jonesy with so many memorable keyboard pieces and unsurpassable bass playing. So, if I were going to write a book about John, how would it be possible without delving into the vault of memories of a great friend and musician 'Jonesy'?

It had been years since I had seen John but I was able to contact him through his manager Richard Chadwick, who kindly set up a meeting so I could find out what happened between Middlesborough and Scandinavia. The meeting was to take place at Richard's office in Portland Road and, as it was such a beautiful day, I decided to walk the short distance from Debbie's studio. As I ventured down Ladbroke Grove, memories flooded back of when our kid would bring the latest album test pressing home and would be so excited about another new sound Jonesy had come up with. Whether it was the melotron beginning to 'Stairway To Heaven', the punchy start to 'Trampled Underfoot' or 'No Quarter's' quite beautiful piano sound. Whatever, it would be greeted with, "Listen to this, listen to this", as Jimmy peeled off another great guitar solo. John was always in awe of the musical gifts of John Paul Jones and Jimmy Page. There are certain pieces of music that will always stir a memory and 'No Quarter' does it for me. I remember myself and wife Lin had been invited to John and Pat's one night for dinner, back in the early 70s while they were still living in Hagley. It was a warm, still evening and we decided to go for a swim in the pool. After a while John decided he wanted to play a track for us all, so he and Pat went into the house, leaving Lin and me alone in the pool. Then through the quiet night air came this unbelievable piano playing, sounding as if it was being played underwater. What a classic piece!

Daydreaming aside, I arrived at the office, but in true Zep style John hadn't. It wasn't long before Jonesy came in and bugger me, he didn't look any older. It was great to see him again and it was soon decided that we should go to the pub to do the interview. We found a table outside, purchased some refreshments and then went back in time. "Well John, tell me *your* version of how it all started."

"I rang Jimmy when I read he was going to form a new band, because I was doing sessions at the time, and I asked him if he needed a bass player. He told me he was going up to Birmingham to see a singer who knows a drummer and that we might have a band by the time he gets back," he recalls of how he finally jumped aboard the Zeppelin express. "When he got back he rang me to say that John was playing with Tim Rose, and at that time, I think, he was making either £100 a week; or was it £40? Anyway, could we top it? John didn't really want to leave Rosy because he thought it was steady work so it took a lot of time and trouble to get him to leave.

"The first time I ever met John was in a tiny basement room we had rented in Lyle Street. We just had loads of amps and speaker cabs there that had been begged, borrowed or stolen and it was literally, 'This is Robert, this is John'.

'How do you do? What shall we do now?'

'What do you know?'

"I'd said I'd been playing sessions and knew nothing at all so Page just said, 'Well I don't know, do you know any Yardbirds songs?' And we went with 'Train Kept A Rollin' in E, and he counted us in and there was like this instant explosion and an instant recognition that this would be a really good outfit to be with. The first thing to strike me about Bonzo was his confidence, and you know he was a real cocky bugger in those days. Still, you have to be to play like that. It was great, instant concentration. He wasn't showing off, but was just aware of what he could do. He was just rock solid."

I had to jump in here and tell Jonesy what Tim had told me about John's timing being erratic in the early days. What did he think? "I never saw John play with Tim, but I suggest you look elsewhere in that band for poor timing. John was rock solid and because drummers and bass players have to work so closely together you soon get to recognise each other's ability. You soon know if you've got a duffer onboard. When you're young and come up through the bands you know immediately, well he's not up to much or my God, I can't work with this bloke. With Bonzo and I, we just listened to each other rather than look at each other and we knew immediately because we were so solid. From the first count in we were absolutely together.

"I must have still been doing some arrangements or had some other commitments left over because, after a short break at rehearsal at Page's house by the river in Pangbourne, I had to go back and finish off a PJ Proby record which I had already done the arrangements for. So to keep the coffers full (because no one was earning any money), I booked all of us onto the session. I told them, 'You know Jimmy and I have this great new drummer you ought to have', and I even got Percy in on tambourine just so he wouldn't feel left out. So our first professional engagement was that PJ Proby record.

"We knew straight away it was going to be good and we would become a great rhythm section. Plus John wasn't influenced by other rock bands. Neither of us really listened to other rock bands. Maybe John did a bit with the Brum bands and he liked The Beatles, but he was more into soul music and loved songs. Funnily enough, I was at the hairdressers this morning when one of the old Delphonics songs came on the radio and I thought of him, as it was a song he used to like. Actually all the best drummers listen to the lyrics, believe it or not, and he always listened to the lyrics. Bonzo would play Beatles songs and many other songs and sing and play drums because all the phrasing has to do with the lyrics. If you ever need to know the words to a song ask the drummer. We also had a love for James Brown and soul music in general. I don't really like rock drummers because they're all a but 'tippy tappy' with nothing really 'booty' underneath and no real understanding of what James Brown called 'The One'. Bonzo did."

Jonesy and I chatted for a long time that afternoon and he told me many funny stories about John and the time they had together, which will appear later on in the book as to fit in with the time they happened. When we arrived back at the office, he had to busy himself signing photos, so sheepishly I asked if I could have one. This he did then put it straight into an envelope. We said our goodbyes then I set off back down Ladbroke Grove. As I walked along the road I took out the photo to have a quick look and was moved by what he had written:

To Mick
Do the lad proud…
John Paul Jones

Three weeks after that initial meeting the boys left this country and headed for Scandinavia, where on the 14 September 1968, and performing under the name The New Yardbirds, Page, Plant, Jones and Bonham took to the stage for the first time. They were away for just over a week playing in Denmark, Sweden and Norway, before hurrying home to record their first album. Time was of the essence as their first UK tour was due to kick off at Surrey University on 15 October, so it was off to Olympic Studios in Barnes, Surrey to record what was basically the playlist from Scandinavia plus a couple of new numbers. The album was produced by Jimmy with help from Glyn Johns, a young rock engineer who had worked with Jimmy on several occasions.

'Led Zeppelin' the first album would only take 30 hours of studio time, from start to finish, and would cost less than £2,000 to produce. I didn't get to see too much of

John during this period, due to him being here, there and everywhere, but when I did catch up with him he was like a kid with a new toy. He was just so excited about the band, the album, the tour and the fact that maybe, just maybe, his dream of making it might be coming true. The band started the tour as The New Yardbirds, but would finish it at London's Fishmonger Hall as Led Zeppelin.

FISHMONGERS HALL
WOOD GREEN
(Fishmongers Arms, 287 High Rd., N.22)
(3 mins. tube)

Friday, Dec., 13th, 7.30
HEADS NIGHT
THE ACTION
plus SUNDAE TIMES
Poetry, Toby & Colin, Films, Guests
EXPLOSIVE SPECTRUM, D.J : JERRY FLOYD
ENVIRONMENT

Friday, December 20th
LED ZEPPELIN
(formerly Yardbirds)

plus by popular demand:
CLOSED CELL SPONGE

Phonographic cylinders, Berwick Street
Musicland

Chapter 9

WHAT NOW? AMERICA!

"I can't say how long Led Zeppelin will last, but we'll go on for as long as we can. When I first joined the group, I didn't know Jimmy, and I felt a bit shy. He was the big star, and had been around for ages with The Yardbirds. Now the group is closer than ever, and there is a lot of scope for all of us."
– John Bonham

While the lads had been working hard, the fifth member of Led Zeppelin had been working even harder. Peter Grant, a rather large Englishman who had learnt his trade through the early 60s as tour manager for a lot of American Rock'n'Roll artists, had come back to this country thanks to the foresight of Don Arden. Peter had also been a wrestler, which gave him an aura, which let people know he knew what he was doing and that he didn't take any shit from anybody. As manager of Led Zeppelin he had flown to New York and secured a very lucrative record deal with Atlantic Records and booked the boys on a tour of the States. They would debut in Denver, Colorado on 26 December.

With only a couple of days to get packed, John was rushing around in a state of excitement. Christmas presents needed to be bought and a heap of other things had to be sorted. The worry of leaving his wife Pat and young son Jason alone over Christmas had taken his mind off his other great worry – flying, a dread he would have for the rest of his life. Still, bags packed and farewells exchanged, John boarded the plane in search for his El Dorado on 23 December. Accompanied by Robert, Jimmy, Jonesy and Peter Grant, they set off for America. Landing in Los Angeles, they were met by Richard Cole, an employee of Peter's who had been working with Vanilla Fudge but was now to become tour manager for Led Zeppelin, a job he would not only do for many years, but also do very well.

Ricardo, as he was known to most, would look after his lads like a shepherd and with his 'I can get you what you want, when you want it' attitude, he soon became an integral part of the band. Cole's job started in earnest on 26 December, when he had to get the band to their first gig at the McNicholls Arena in Denver and then to Boston to play The Tea Party two days later, as support to Vanilla Fudge.

'Drummer Carmine Appice remembers being so impressed with this young English drummer, that he helped secure him a drum sponsorship.'

"John became very close to Carmine Appice when we first toured with Vanilla Fudge," recalls Jonesy. "That's where he got the gong idea from. I became good friends with Tim Bogart because he was such a good bass player. The bastard had only been playing bass for two years when I met him. He'd been a sax player up until then. I could have killed him because he had a bloody good voice too. Anyway, there was this bit in 'Dazed and Confused' where we all stop to let Page and Plant do all the screaming and high bits, then we come back in with the fast riff. Well, we did the stop, then there was the 'Baby, baby, baby' scream stuff and then in came the riff. It's a real hard, fast riff, and when Robert and Jimmy turned round they found Bogart and Appice and not Jones and Bonham. We'd swapped places while they were out front and because we were always in the dark at this point, no one had noticed!"

Carmine Appice (Drummer with Vanilla Fudge and later with Jeff Beck)

Drummer Carmine Appice remembers being so impressed with this young English drummer, that he helped secure him a drum sponsorship. "After watching Bonzo play I called up the Ludwig Drum Co. and said they should endorse this guy John Bonham. Then I sent them the album and said I thought the band was going to be big. So they gave John the endorsement, same kit as mine, gong and all. Two 26″ bass drums, a 12x15 marching tenor drum, a 16x18 and 16x16 floor toms and a 6½″ deep snare drum. All rare sizes in those days. As for the "I think they're gonna be big" – understatement of four decades!

"After getting the endorsement, John and I were testing out some new Ludwig stands while playing at the Kinetic Playground in Chicago. By the end of the night we had both broken the stands so we gave them back and said 'They're gonna need to be a lot stronger, we broke them'. You should have seen the look of shock on the faces of the people from Ludwig.

"It was also John who told Tim and I that Jeff Beck

wanted to form a band with us. That was right after he'd played with Jeff at the Singer Bowl and had taken all his clothes off while playing, which was really wild as my parents were backstage watching the show, which left me trying to explain to them why. What a night!"

The band's first tour of America was scheduled to finish on 8 February in Chicago, but John was very homesick, so while there was a break at the beginning of that month, he took the opportunity to fly home. I had taken over John's job at Osbournes Tailors, a shop which can still be seen in Redditch town centre, albeit under its new name Jazz, so it came as quite a shock when John came marching into the shop to see me on 4 February. He told me he just had to get home to see his family and proceeded to tell me all about the exploits of the previous six weeks during my lunch hour. And then he was gone again. I only saw John a few times that year because Led Zeppelin played 139 gigs throughout 1969, and only 33 of them were here in the UK.

'I only saw John a few times that year because Led Zeppelin played 139 gigs throughout 1969, and only 33 of them were here in the UK.'

On 18 February I received a phone call from John, telling me that he was back home and that he had a copy of their first album. He was so enthusiastic about it all and asked if I'd like to pop over that night to hear it. Of course I did, but I'd made plans to go out. "That's fine," said John. "Bring them all over, we'll have a bit of a party."

By now John and Pat were living in their own flat on Eve Hill in Dudley, West Midlands and as I'd arranged, I picked up my friends and headed over to Dudley. The one thing that worried me slightly was that me and my three mates were well into our soul music, and although I hadn't heard any of the album, I knew it wouldn't be soul. We arrived at the flat around 8.30pm and once all the introductions were over with, Pat took young Jason to bed, John poured everyone a glass of wine, then on went Led Zep 1. For the first couple of tracks we just sat there giving quizzical sideways glances at each other, as John eagerly gave a running commentary of who was doing what on each track. Slowly we warmed to the record. It gave Robert a platform to do what he did best, sing some raunchy blues. There was quite brilliant guitar work from Jimmy, some of those haunting Jonesy intros and it was all held together by John's skill on the drums. I think it was John's total enthusiasm for the band, the music and the unbelievable time he'd spent in America that really made me start to enjoy the work. Over the next couple of hours we drank wine and listened to his stories of touring the States, being able to play with such great bands as Vanilla Fudge, Iron Butterfly and the MC5. But ultimately it was the fact that by the end of the tour, the band had made the breakthrough they desired. They were the band that everyone was talking about.

June Harris of the *New Musical Express* had this to say: 'The biggest happening of the 1969 heavy rock scene is Led Zeppelin! The reaction to the group's first tour here, currently in progress, has not only been incredible, it's been nothing short of sensational.'

As that evening came to a close John told me he was hiring the Lafayette Club in Wolverhampton the following Monday, because he was throwing a party for Pat's 21st. The band would be coming up to play and did we all want to go? John saw us out and as we were getting into the car he shouted, "Oi! What d'yer think of the new motor?" pointing to a beautiful black S-Type Jaguar and grinning large. "Bostin', innit!"

Chapter 10

PARTY PARTY!

As John was making arrangements for the party I was busy at work kitting myself out with a new suit, shirt and tie, ready for the big occasion. Come 7.30pm on the night of Monday 24 February 1969, I picked up Jacko and then set off for John's flat in Dudley, calling for friends Alf and Sheila along the way. From John's we set off for the club in the comfort of the new Jag. It seemed like a rather good start to what was to be a great night. Little did I know what was in store!

The party itself was a great success. The place was full of friends and family so I spent most of the night dancing with Pat's sister, Beryl and friends Ros, Jill and Joyce until the highlight of the night was about to commence. John took to the stage along with Jimmy, Robert and John Paul and they stunned the audience with some superb music. Like me, most people present had not seen the band before and were all as amazed as I was. I felt so proud of John. After all those years of traipsing around Brum it had finally happened for him. They left the stage to thunderous applause and everyone rushed to congratulate John and the rest of the boys.

The following Saturday, Led Zeppelin started their second UK tour, consisting of seven gigs, starting at the Fishmongers Hall in London. As soon as they finished their last date, they flew to Scandinavia to do another seven appearances, including a Danish TV show in Copenhagen. Then it was back to Britain to finish off the tour. When they arrived back, it was into the Maida Vale Studio in London, to record for the BBC World Service, and then do their first TV appearance on the BBC show *How Late It Is.* On 22 March Led Zeppelin were booked to play at Mothers in Brum, so John phoned me to tell me to come along and see them, as it would be the only local gig on the tour. For Robert and John it would be a great return to their roots, as it would also be their first gig in Birmingham together since their Band Of Joy days.

Mothers had been a long established venue for live music, situated above two shops in the Erdington High Street and had originally been called the Carlton Ballroom. It became the Carlton Club when Phil Myatt and associates took it over in 1963 and was a regular haunt for John throughout the mid-60s. With the direction of music changing, thus did the Carlton. With its name change to Mothers, it became one of the great progressive rock venues, playing host to the likes of Fleetwood Mac, The Who, Pink Floyd and Chicken Shack, to name but a few. Tonight it was the turn of Led Zeppelin, and with John and Robert back on home soil and in front of a lot of old friends there was no stopping them. The place was packed and as the band launched into their opening number the venue erupted. The end result of course, was a great night for band and audience.

In April, Zeppelin flew back to the States for a second tour. This time they were a headline act and earning a darn sight more money. There would be 28 shows, ending on John's 21st birthday at the Filmore East in New York. Upon their return to Britain, their album had entered the Billboard Top Ten and they were dubbed the new Cream and heroes of British Rock. Within a week they'd begun a fourth tour of the UK and appeared on John Peel's *Top Gear* radio show and *Rock Hour* for the BBC, recorded at the Playhouse Theatre in London. I followed the tour by reading whatever bits I could find in the music press and waiting anxiously for 28 June, when I would accompany John to the Bath Festival.

On previous occasions I had travelled to gigs either on my scooter or on the bus, but this time it would be in style, to what had been advertised as the 'Big One'. We drove down during the morning, meeting up with Jimmy, Robert and John Paul in the back stage bar. It was pretty unreal for me, rubbing shoulders with some of the great musicians I had only read about, like Fleetwood Mac, Ten Years After and the man who'd launched so many great names from his Bluesbreakers, Mr John Mayall.

The Recreation Ground and Pavilion was in a lovely setting in the centre of Bath, and on a warm summer's afternoon I couldn't think of anywhere I would rather be, along with 12,000 other people. I had taken a camera with me so, well before Zeppelin was to go on, I made my way out into the crowd and towards the front of the stage. Finding a nice patch of grass, I waited patiently for the emergence of Led Zeppelin. When the band took to the stage the audience surged past me, leaving me only enough time to take three photos before I was swallowed up by 'The Ocean'. As the show finished and the crowd moved back, I was still on the floor, looking like one of those hedgehogs you see squashed on the road.

After the show it was a few beers in the bar and then back home, via the local fish and chip shop of course. Watching the band that afternoon, one could really notice how that second tour of the States had honed the band into a really sharp outfit oozing confidence. The press declared, 'Zeppelin's fiery set in which they played their own individual form of progressive blues devastated most and proved one of the most enjoyable sets of the festival.'

On 5 July, the onslaught of America resumed, this time playing large stadiums and open-air concerts. The highlight of this tour, for John at least, was to be able to play at the Newport Jazz Festival alongside one of his heroes and major influences, James Brown and his Band. On the 6th, roles were reversed, Zeppelin would take the stage, and The James Brown Band in turn would stand and watch them.

"I've seen all three James Brown drummers stand round him at the Newport Festival in disbelief," recalls Jonesy. "Wondering how one guy does what all three of them did."

After all the times John had played James Brown records on jukeboxes in clubs and cafés, he was finally up there playing the same venue.

Apart from a short break at home in September, two gigs in France and a one off appearance at London's Lyceum

'Led Zeppelin 2', which had been released in America in October, had knocked The Beatles' 'Abbey Road' off the top of the Billboard album chart.'

Ballroom, John and his compatriots spent what was left of 1969 touring the States. The year finished on a high when, just after 16 months together, they were awarded one Gold and two Platinum discs for sales in America, by the then Parliamentary Secretary to the Board of Trade, Mrs Gwyneth Dunwoody. Led Zeppelin had sold 100,000 albums in the UK and over $5million worth in America. After a family Christmas at home, news came through on 27 December that 'Led Zeppelin 2', which had been released in America in October, had knocked The Beatles' 'Abbey Road' off the top of the Billboard album chart.

Chapter 11

IN PERSON, LED ZEPPELIN INTO THE 70s

With all the hard work and hard touring of 1969 came the spoils. John had moved out of the flat in Dudley and purchased a nice sized detached house in Hagley, a quiet village some ten miles east of Birmingham, and was busy decorating it when it was time to go back on the road. Not so much a jaunt this time, as they were opening their third UK tour just up the road at Birmingham Odeon on 7 January. Although Debbie was just eight years old, there was no way she was going to be left at home, so Mum decided she could come and Jacko and I met them and Pat at the venue. It would be Mum and Debbie's first time seeing John playing with Zep and by the end of the show they were both stunned. A couple of old faces also turned up to catch the show, Matt Maloney and Move bassist Ace Kefford. We all got to see John's full drum solo, then titled 'Pat's Delight' but later renamed 'Moby Dick' for the second album. John received three standing ovations that night and the look on Jacko and Mum's faces was a picture. Eyes filled with tears of pride as they realised, watching their son take the deserved acclaim, that all the arguments, pranged vans and other escapades had all been worth it. The set finished with a Rock'n'Roll medley that got everyone dancing in the aisles and into such fervour that they only let the band finish after four encores.

'It isn't hard to understand the substantial appeal of Led Zeppelin,' wrote Nick Logan in the *New Musical Express* (NME). 'Their current two hour blitzkrieg of musically perfected hard rock that combines heavy dramatics with lashings of sex into a formula that can't fail to move senses and limbs. At the pace they've been setting on their current seven town British tour there are few groups who could live with them.'

As the tour carried on around Britain, Jacko and I were

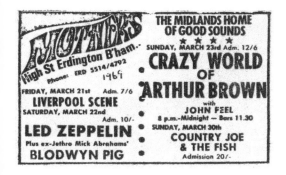

Opposite
Led Zeppelin perform at the Bath Festival

doing the carpentry at John's and he himself, when he wasn't playing, would do the decorating. Feeling that he had worked very hard he decided to treat himself to a new Rolls Royce and then took Jack and me to the Cross Keys pub nearby. During the break between the UK tour and departing for Scandinavia we sorted out all the other work that needed doing at his new house. I was to put a large panel fence around the garden, which was about 100 yards long, while Jacko replaced the doors. It was decided the work should start while John was away on their first European tour. Although his life was moving at a fast pace, he hadn't forgotten about his old mate and roadie Matt Maloney, and had asked him to leave his job and start working for him exclusively. Matthew didn't need asking twice. On 2 March John left for Europe, taking Pat with him for a short holiday and I went to the house to meet Matt so we could sort out the fencing. As a driver and roadie Matt was second to none, but as a manual worker I'd have got more help if I'd phoned the Samaritans, but with a lot of hard graft and the odd sneaky trip out in the Roller we managed to get the job done.

The beginning of the 70s saw Jacko and I living above a ladies hairdressers in Studley, Warwickshire overlooking the Duke Of Marlborough Pub and a couple of doors down from the Studley Conservative Club. John would get away from the hustle and bustle of the rock scene by coming over for a quiet drink and a game of snooker with us at the club and then crossing over the road for some George Rafters at the Duke. Some years later a film crew would besiege the Con Club to film one of John's scenes in the film *The Song Remains the Same*, but it was to the Duke that he came after the American tour, where we all had a drink and listened in awe to his stories. He looked very tired as he told us that the tour had been a tremendous success though there had been a lot of trouble between fans and over-eager riot police. There had also been one occasion where a guy had pulled a gun on them after a run-in at a restaurant, which prompted them to hire several bodyguards to accompany them through the Deep South. On a brighter note though, Led Zeppelin had been made honorary citizens of Memphis, Tennessee.

Time simply shot by as we listened intently. Not that it particularly mattered, as the landlord of the Duke, Gordon Scutt, one of the most genial men I have ever met, was the partner of our Aunty Mary, which meant licensing laws weren't really adhered to as far as we were concerned. We didn't have any of that silly, "Can you drink up now please". So, some time after the bewitching hour, John decided it would be a really good idea to have a beer-drinking race. The rules were that we would both drink pints of mild and the odds were to be 100/1. Being a heavy gambler, I placed £1 on me to win. Just over four seconds later I was a hundred quid better off and feeling quite pleased with myself, but then John changed the rules. "It's the best of three," he said ordering the next round. Again, a few seconds later I was two hundred quid better off. What amazed both of us was that, on the second round, Gordon had joined in with a pint of gin and tonic and had only lost by a couple of seconds. John decided to call a halt to the festivities on account that I was now earning more than he was.

Two months passed before I saw John again. This time he had arranged to pick me up on his way to the Bath Festival on 28 June. Both John and Matthew had decided to have a night out in Brum prior to driving down to the gig, so I had gone off to a party to get in the right mood for Bath. At 3.00am in the morning the impatient honking of a car horn told me my lift had arrived. This time we would travel in another of John's acquisitions, a sleek new Jensen Interceptor which Matthew was driving so that John could get some sleep on the back seat, along with a case of Dom Perignon champagne just in case we got thirsty on the trip. Within a couple of minutes John passed round the refreshments, a bottle each to start with, so the music volume was turned up and we roared off into the night.

This was the life. The purr of a powerful engine with a bottle of champers in your hand whilst reclining in soft cream leather, noticing the speedometer clock top 150mph. Somehow, with one hand on the steering wheel and the other clasping his bottle, Matthew managed to fly us down to Bristol. As dawn was breaking through the

Above
John Bonham adding another
car to his collection

night sky, we arrived feeling rough and looking worse. That year's event had become so big that the show had been moved from Bath to the Showgrounds at Shepton Mallet, some 20 miles south of the original venue. After a few wrong turns we finally found the sanctuary of the artiste's compound with one thing on our mind; getting into the caravan allocated for Led Zep and getting some shut eye. Things didn't look good when we found the van locked with someone asleep inside. After some serious banging on the door a sleepy voice told us to "Fuck off". Failing to see the funny side, John instructed us to tip the whole thing over. As the caravan tilted at 45 degrees the door was finally swung open by a rough looking Richard Cole. In the van behind him were some even rougher looking women.

Everyone settled down inside and I was sent in search of some breakfast. As I mooched around in search of a burger van, or anything that sold food, I took the opportunity to sneak up on to the stage to be greeted by a sight that made me feel very small. It looked like something from The Alamo, with bodies lying everywhere, wrapped in sleeping bags or huddled together under blankets and sat around camp fires that gave off whisps of smoke, lending the whole scene the feel of a battlefield. The previous year's festival had been big, but not as big as this. It was simply awe-inspiring. Remembering the job in hand, I carried on with my search until I had mustered four sad looking sandwiches and six bottles of beer, then returned to the van.

I would spend most of the day ensconced in the caravan meeting all the people who came to chat with the members of Led Zeppelin. As was Peter Grant's way, the van soon filled up with food and drink so his boys wouldn't go hungry. There was a party atmosphere all day as the likes of Frank Zappa, Julie Felix, and Donovan and many other musicians, from all the bands lined up for the second day of the festival, popped in for a drink. This line-up included Jefferson Airplane, the Moody Blues, The Byrd's, Frank Zappa and the Mothers of Invention, Santana and of course Led Zeppelin. I didn't get much chance to see many of the bands because I was busy inventing the word 'liggin', though I made sure I was on the right side of the stage as one of my heroes took to the stage – Carlos Santana and how good they were, providing a superb set that met with great approval from the crowd.

Peter had decided he wanted the band to go on stage at about 7.00pm so that during their performance the sun would set behind them, giving the stage a beautiful glow. I found a spot on the side of the stage then along with about 150,000 other people, awaited the emergence of Led Zeppelin. It was obvious when they did appear, that this was what the crowd had been waiting for and a huge roar echoed around the Somerset countryside. A quick clothes change as John came past (I had to give him my sleeveless jumper because he was going to be too hot in what he was wearing).

They opened the show with 'The Immigrant Song' and went straight into 'Heartbreaker' and then enjoyed the sunset during 'Dazed And Confused', by which time they had the entire crowd on their side. 'Since I've Been Loving You' stunned the crowd into silence, ready for the acoustic set. As the band upped a few gears for 'What Is and What Should Never Be', John's 'Moby Dick' followed to thunderous applause. 'How Many More Times' proved to be the pinnacle, littered with many rock classics, after which the audience made it clear there was no way they were going to let the band leave the stage. So, tambourines were thrown into the sea of fans and the band proceeded with about five encores. Whilst this rock melee continued, I became aware of a very attractive girl standing next to me and after a quick introduction it was decided that we should have a glass of wine back at the caravan. As we were acquainting ourselves, Ricardo burst in saying he had a bottle of gin and I should nip out and get a few tonics from the beer tent. Despite my ears still ringing from Zep's set, I still managed to hear the door lock behind me. What a putz! That bloody Cole's got the girl again! When John arrived on the scene, having noticed me disappear with the girl from the stage, he asked where she'd gone. I told him the story to which he promptly kicked my arse then told me who she was. I can't mention names as to avoid embarrassment to her and her family, but as the song goes, 'her daddy's rich and her momma's good looking'.

Long after the band had left the stage the crowd were still chanting for them, which meant nobody wanted to go on next and follow them. In the end it was the newly formed Hot Tuna, featuring ex-Jefferson Airplane members Jack Casady and Jorma Kaukonen, who did the honours and they did it well. Back at the van, the after-show party was drawing to a close and John asked if I'd mind sleeping in the car and looking after his wage packet. I duly obliged, and as I sat there behind the wheel of the Jensen, with a few readies stashed away under the soft leather seats, a young girl tapped on the window and asked if she could shelter from the rain. Of course, being a gentleman, what else could I say? "Too bloody right you can." As she sat there trying to get dry, I can remember thinking, 'this is the life, this really is the li... ZZzzzzzzzzz.' Doh!

Some two weeks after the Bath festival, according to many books, the band played a short tour of Germany and it has been widely reported that on 11 July, at the Festhalle in Frankfurt, they broke the record for the largest audience for a single rock group in Germany, by playing to 11,000 fans. Wrong! On that particular date John was helping break another attendance record at St. Mary's Parish Church's annual summer fayre in Studley, Warwickshire. The Rev David Acheson had recruited John's help after they'd met several times at the Duke of Marlborough. It was John's job to help raise money by signing autographs and judging the Queen of the Fayre contest. An added bonus was that John had got Atlantic Records to send some 100 assorted albums so that they could sell at knock down prices to help raise more money for charity. After the event, we joined the Vicar of Studley for a spot of refreshments back at the 'Duke', emerging in the early hours of the following day.

Less than one month later, Led Zeppelin started their sixth American tour in Cincinnati on 5 August. This time, however, a minimum fee of $25,000 per show was

"The atmosphere was fantastic, when you consider it was cold and windy. And even when it rained they sat through it and could still be happy. I didn't think you could get an atmosphere like that at a concert."
– John Bonham after the Bath Festival

the going rate, but 35 performances later, when they played at New York's Madison Square Garden, they would receive over $100,000 for their performance. It was during this tour that the fans back home in England would vote them the most popular rock band, knocking The Beatles off the top spot in the *Melody Maker* Reader's National Poll. Then, on 5 October 'Led Zeppelin 3' was released. With over 700,00 advanced orders in the States alone, it topped the album charts on both sides of the Atlantic. Within two months the band were back at work on their next album at Island Studios in London, but after a short Christmas break, all rehearsals and recording were moved to Headley Grange, a rambling country house in Hampshire.

Chapter 12

1971 – A RETURN TO THE CLUBS

Interview with Chris Welch at time of Zep IV release.

"I can't say what we are going to sound like in the future, and I don't really want to know. If I could tell you what we're going to sound like in two years time it would ruin it anyway. We might be on top next year, or I might be back on the buildings." – John Bonham

With the basic recording of the fourth album completed, Led Zeppelin kicked off their British tour on 5 March at the Ulster Hall in Belfast. John had driven over to Northern Ireland, aided by Mathew, who would choose this night to make his first major fuck up! After a memorable gig, both for the band as it was their first visit to Northern Ireland, and the audience, who rarely got to see any British bands due to the troubles, it was Mathew's job to drive John to Dublin. However, he took a wrong turn and ended up in the Falls Road – a total no-go area. The road was littered with glass and any other object deemed worthy to be thrown at the armoured cars.

"Hey mate, what do you think I should do?" Mathew asked calmly.

"Get us the fuck out of here!" John replied, not so calmly.

And so, Mathew drove straight through and eventually arrived safely at Dublin's Intercontinental Hotel.

It was to be reported by Richard Cole, at a later date, that on this particular night, Mathew assaulted the hotel's chef and Richard had broken John's nose with a single punch. Knowing both John and Mathew like I do, I have to admit that I find these claims a trifle hard to swallow. But, as we have learnt over the decades, if it's

"The band just goes from strength to strength. I keep thinking we're going to wake up one morning and find it's all over. Sure we've had criticism. When we first came up we were called a second Cream, but now you see they call some new groups a second Zeppelin."
– John Bonham

been written about Led Zeppelin then of course it must be true!

During the break between the UK tour and flying off to Europe for their second tour, John and Pat came over to the flat to see me and Jacko. With that usual grin plastered across his face he told me he'd brought my birthday present a couple of months early as he would be in Europe on my 21st. He then proceeded to hand me an envelope which I assumed was my birthday card, but which to my surprise contained the log book for a brand new MGB sports car which he had parked round the corner. After flying around town a dozen times or so, I picked up Lin and we all went to the Duke for a premature birthday party.

Led Zeppelin started that second tour of Europe in the first week of June in Copenhagen, Denmark. The 25th and final date of the tour was at Milan's Vigorelli Velodrome on 5 July. Sadly that would end in total disaster as heavy-handed police fired tear gas into the audience every time they stood up to cheer. Eventually the crowd fought back. The police retaliated by bombarding them with tear gas and the band had to escape down a tunnel and lock themselves in the dressing room. When they were finally allowed back out they found the stage wrecked and all the equipment destroyed. John's drum technician Mick Hinton had stayed behind in an attempt to save some gear but ended up being taken to hospital with bad cuts to his head from a broken bottle. A very subdued Led Zeppelin flew back to England.

With hardly any respite, the group played two warm-up shows at the Casino in Montreaux, Switzerland, before undertaking a 22-date tour of North America. After the last concert in Honolulu the band holidayed in Hawaii, relaxing in the knowledge that they had just grossed over $1million. Surely they were the biggest band in the world?

From there it was on to their first ever tour of Japan, during which they played a charity concert in Hiroshima for the victims of the atomic bomb. Afterwards the Mayor of Hiroshima presented the band with a letter of appreciation and the city peace medal. I recall a highly amusing anecdote John told me from the tour. At one of the gigs, a young Japanese lad was to introduce the band but was having a bit of a problem pronouncing the band's name. When John arrived in the dressing room the poor chap was sat in front of the mirror repeating the name over and over again.

"Red Leppelin. No. Led Reppelin. No."

Each time he got it wrong he became more and more angry. With less than half an hour to go before showtime he finally and triumphantly got it right.

'Another achievement John didn't mention was their ability to re-arrange several hotel rooms using Samurai swords. That, along with other antics, saw Led Zeppelin banned from the Tokyo Hilton. For life.'

"Led Zeppelin," he chirped, jumping for joy. And with the show finally upon them so the young man took his position to announce to the waiting crowd…

"Ladies and gentlemen, Red Repperin! Arrgghhh!"

OSAKA, JAPAN, 29 September.

During the acoustic set, the band noticed that Bonzo had disappeared. Robert decided to talk a little more in hope that John would return.

"Where's Bonzo… Bonzoooo. Mr Bonham. Come on, shout after three – Mr Bonhammmmmmmm". Jimmy started laughing. The audience continued shouting and applauding for John. From Robert's tone, you could tell he was starting to get annoyed. Swearing both at the road crew and the audience, he says, "What can you say, Mr Bonham goes to the bar with the geisha girl."

They play 'That's The Way'. John still hasn't appeared. After a few more shouts from Robert and the audience, he finally turns up to applause and loud cheers. The fact is that John (together with the rest of the band) had the worst case of diarrhoea. The rest of the concert continued as scheduled, but the toilet was in charge of John, even as they headed home.

"It was a fantastic place to play," John remembered. "Rock music only started to really happen there a few years ago, but it's now the second biggest market in the world. The people were so friendly and we had the best rock promoter in the world there looking after us. It turned out the 'Immigrant Song' is one of our biggest favourites in Japan, and it's the number we always open with. So the audiences were going potty right from the start."

Another achievement John didn't mention was their ability to re-arrange several hotel rooms using Samurai swords. That, along with other antics, saw Led Zeppelin banned from the Tokyo Hilton. For life.

Towards the end of the year, to coincide with the release of the fourth album, the band undertook another tour of Britain. As Messrs, Page, Plant, Jones and Bonham traversed the motorways of England, so did I. The only difference was that I was doing it in an old box van, working for a haulage company from Redditch. On 27 November I joined up with John and we headed north to Preston, where the band were appearing at the Town Hall.

I watched the show perched on the stairs leading to the stage and, as the performance reached its climax, Mick Hinton came over and said that John wanted a pint of mild and wanted me to fetch it for him. When I returned from the bar I was instructed to take it over to the side of the drum kit. I crouched down and tried to get there without being noticed, before trying to place the beer near John from behind a speaker cabinet. Like lightening John grabbed my arm, pointed to a set of congas behind his kit and shouted "Play them". Before I could reply "How?" the opening riff for 'Whole Lotta Love' had kicked in. So there I was stranded and thinking how not to look like a prat, so I started to play. Though I say so myself, I thought I was doing okay. Okay until I looked up and saw a sea of faces looking back at me. At this moment my arms went into overdrive and my legs decided they weren't with me and wanted to leave. As the number came to a close all I could think of was getting the hell off that stage, but John and Robert had other ideas, escorting me to the front of the stage to take a bow alongside Jimmy and John Paul. After beating a hasty retreat to the bar, John looked at me while I was still visibly shaken, grinned and said, "Good, ain't it!"

Although scared shitless, that night would remain one of the great memories of my life. The down side of this event was that it was an extra date added on after the original tour dates had been confirmed, so the gig was never written about and there were no photos, and to make things worse, it was about the only gig not to be recorded on bootleg. So if there is anyone out there who was at that gig with a camera and has a photo of me stood alongside 'our kid' and the rest of the band, can you please send me one?

A few days later, while trying to get my old box van round the streets of Leeds with Bob Atcheson as co-pilot, we decided to take a small detour to see Zep play in Manchester at the Belle View. The evening was going really well until I realised the show was almost over and I remembered what had happened in Preston. This time the legs won and I was off and didn't stop until I was firmly locked inside one of the venue's toilet cubicles. I finally resurfaced when I heard the music finish and the crowd roar. Of course, I hadn't anticipated the fact that as I'd be trying to make my way backstage, thousands of people would be walking in the opposite direction. By the time I arrived Mick Hinton informed me that John was already on his way back to the Elbow Room in Brum and was a little miffed that I hadn't got up to do the number. If that wasn't bad enough, bloody Bob had gone with him, along with the keys to my van and all my money. Luckily for me, Robert lent me £10 on the agreement that, "If you spend it, okay, but if you don't, give it back!" Obviously spending it was foremost on my mind, so I checked into a nice hotel and the following day purchased Van Morrison's 'Moondance' and 'Tupelo Honey'. Ta Robert. Sorted!

It was a shame that the only person to suffer through this crisis would be Mathew, who had been dispatched, post haste, back to Manchester to return the keys and would have to sleep in the car and await my return the next day. Thanks mate.

In February of 1972 Led Zeppelin embarked on their one and only tour of Australia and New Zealand, playing to sell-out crowds in Perth, Adelaide, Melbourne, Auckland, Sydney and finishing in Brisbane.

"I remember a nice thing I did with Bonzo when we were coming back from Australia," recalls John Paul Jones. "We had played Sydney and a few other places and then we had to catch a plane from Brisbane to Sydney and then fly from Sydney straight back to England. The plane was very early in the morning, we had stayed up all night. I don't know where the others were but Bonzo and I ended up in a bar with all these Fijians. They looked like a sort of rugby team and they were all lounging about obviously waiting for the same plane. So we started chatting and drinking and it turned out they were the Fijian Police Choir, who had also just done a gig in Brisbane. After a couple more drinks, of course music came up and they started singing for us. There's me and Bonzo sitting there, beers all around us and there's six or seven of them, big buggers they were, and they start the sweetest singing. All these beautiful old Fijian songs. It was lovely stuff and we all sat around having a great time. Then they told us it was our turn.

"I said 'Hold on, he's a drummer and I'm a bass player.'

"They said 'Well, you must be able to sing something.'

"So Bonzo and I looked at each other and thought 'Ah, I know' and we went through half the 1959 Everly's repertoire. We did 'Love Hurts', 'So Sad', 'Dream' and we did 'Wake Up Little Susie'. It was hilarious serenading the Fijian Police Choir with Everly Brothers songs. It had been a great night and as we parted they gave us presents of necklaces and Koweri shells."

It was also during this tour that John met up with Mum's sister Aunt Dorothy, who he had not seen for nearly 15 years after she'd emigrated to New Zealand in the late 50s. They caught up with each other at the gig in Auckland and he gave her the Gold LP for 'Led Zeppelin', he'd received for Australian sales.

(Interview with Chris Welch at time of Zep IV release.)

Chapter 13

THE SEARCH FOR THE OLD HYDE

During the breaks of '72 John was on the look out for a new home. Somewhere in the country, and with a fair bit of land. On several occasions Jacko and I went with him to look over some of the properties, and eventually he found what he was looking for; The Old Hyde Farm, situated in Cutnall Green, Worcestershire. Perched on top of a hill overlooking the Worcestershire countryside, John had visualised what he wanted to do with the place. The house would be virtually knocked down and then rebuilt to about twice the size, but most importantly, the farm would be developed and would become workable once more. Jacko was to oversee the project and do all the carpentry and was also to put a team together to do all the work needed to complete the building. A friend of Jacko's, Stan Blick, was brought in to do all the brickwork with his son Pete and the first job was to repair all the farm buildings and renew the cottage, so a farm manager could move in and start to get things back in order. It would take just over two years to complete and would be the subject of more than one humorous occurrence. But it would also preside over two very sad incidents.

Also purchased at this time was *The Boston Strangler*, a hot rod that had once belonged to Jeff Beck. It was a Model T Ford powered by a bloody big engine, and owing to the lack of silencers sounded like a den of lions fighting over breakfast. On one of the early outings for the rod John and I took it for a spin down the Hagley Road to the Bromsgrove dual carriageway, which was a perfect test track for all new motors, and were suddenly surrounded by about 20 large blokes on even larger motorbikes. As they pulled alongside I saw John make a quick sign of the cross on his chest and shoot me a look that said 'We're gonna get our arses kicked here', but at that very moment, their leader raised his fist in the air and shouted "Great motor Bonzo" and they all sped

Previous page
John Bonham escaping from the pressures of
touring at the helm of *The Staysea*

Above
Cigarette, cigar and beer,
Bonham winds down

away. Thank God for recognition! Within ten minutes we were involved in another fracas, when a car full of loud lads drove past hurling abuse at us. The final straw came when one of the idiots shouted, "Who sold you that? Mickey Mouse?" John rammed the gear stick down a gear or two and banged the accelerator to the floor. With an explosion of sound the front wheels leaped off the ground and *The Boston Strangler* leapt into action. Ooooh shit! As we went past the offending motor like a bat out of hell, the impact caused such a panic that they ended up on the central reservation, and that's where we left them.

Whether it was the childhood memories of Jacko's boat, or the fact that The Old Hyde was only five miles from Stourport-on-Severn, in April he took delivery of *The Staysea*, a 34-feet sea-going cabin cruiser that was to be moored in Stourport. After a couple of days of cleaning and getting the boat spotless, John decided that a cruise down the river was in order. Large quantities of food and *Newcastle Brown Ale* were stowed away and John, Mathew and I set off down the river to Worcester. With memories of Jerome K Jerome's famous tale of 'Three Men in a Boat' running riot in my head we approached the first lock on the river. Unfortunately for us, any further thoughts of the tales of the nineteenth century author were curtailed because the lock keeper disputed ownership of the boat and wouldn't let us through. In the end we had to make do with a cruise up and down a three-mile stretch of the river until all the provisions had been disposed of.

That short break well and truly over, John returned to the studio in May and began an eighth American tour in June. A second tour of Japan, the Tokyo Hilton notwithstanding, followed in October, and then two quick shows in Montreaux before a triumphant Led Zeppelin returned to undertake their largest ever tour of Britain. Eighteen different venues and 120,000 tickets would sell out in one day.

Chapter 14

ZEPPELIN TAKE TRENTHAM GARDENS

"I'm still the same person. I enjoy decorating and gardening, and I'm still as hot-headed as ever. I'm a bit quick tempered. I never sit down and think about things. I couldn't do what Jimmy does and shut myself away in the country.
I like people around me all the time. Parties, going out and general looning. I suppose I'm a bit of a noisy person. In fact I'm probably the noisiest of the four of us."
– John Bonham

John had chosen a beautiful position for his new home, The Old Hyde Farm. Set on the brow of a hill overlooking the village, the main house and the farm buildings needed a great deal of renovation and construction work. That wasn't a problem. John got down to designing it with a little help from Jacko ("You can't bloody do that there, the whole lot will bloody fall down.") and a lovely young architect called Grace Plant ("Yes John, that's no problem, if that's what you want we can do it."), the plans soon came together and work was well under way. Having Grace around added a touch of glamour to the site, and, as you can imagine, none of us blokes were about to complain. Anyway, it was sort of keeping it in the family as Grace was married to one of Robert's cousins, Malcolm, who was an insurance salesman and guess what? He supplied us with all the insurance we needed.

John wanted the farm cottage and outbuildings to be finished first, so that the farm could be up and running as soon as possible. He wanted to rear a pedigree herd of Hereford cattle, better known as 'Herfuds' to us country ass boys. To achieve this, he needed a farm manager, barns, stables and other assorted buildings, which is why Jacko and I were out in the bloody cold, renewing the old farm buildings. John tried to spend as many hours during the day as he could with us whilst work was in progress. Inevitably, however, the hours started to dwindle and it wasn't long before John's visits were only fleeting. The reason? Led Zeppelin were on their sixth UK tour.

It had started at the end of November 1972 and now, two months later in January the following year, the band was half way through.

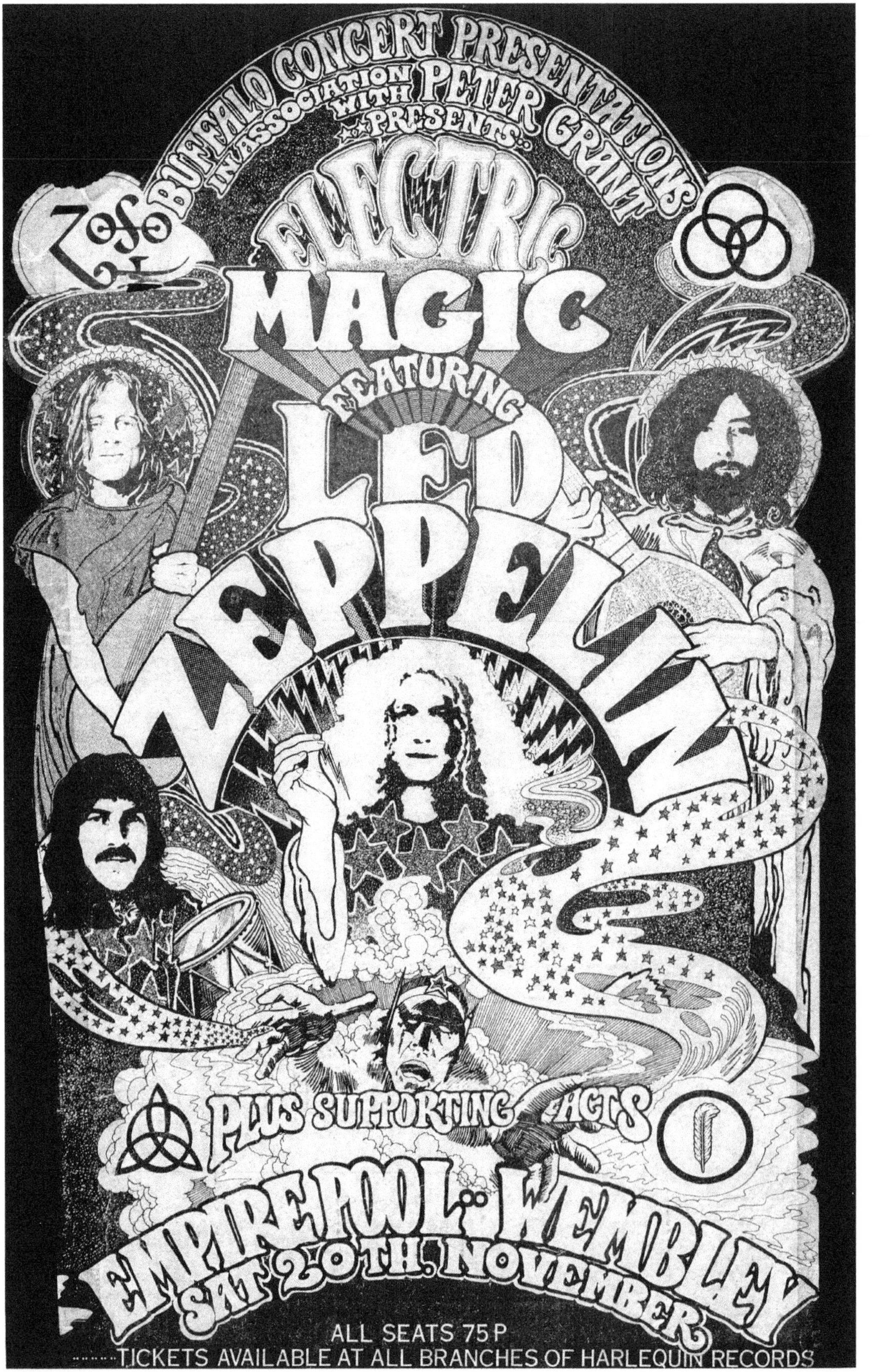
BUFFALO CONCERT PRESENTATIONS
IN ASSOCIATION WITH PETER GRANT
PRESENTS
ELECTRIC
MAGIC
FEATURING
LED ZEPPELIN
PLUS SUPPORTING ACTS
EMPIRE POOL WEMBLEY
SAT 20TH. NOVEMBER
ALL SEATS 75 P
TICKETS AVAILABLE AT ALL BRANCHES OF HARLEQUIN RECORDS

On this particular night they were playing in Stoke-on-Trent, just north of Birmingham, at a place called Trentham Gardens. John had popped in to see if Jacko and I would be all right getting there on our own, because he'd got to go early to do the usual soundchecks. While he was with us he told us about the previous night's gig at the Liverpool Empire. According to John, it had been great because Robert's voice was back to full force, after losing it to flu whilst the band had played Sheffield's City Hall on 2 January. They'd had to cancel a couple of gigs however, but now Robert was fully recovered it was business as usual.

Once travel plans for the evening had been established, John was eager to get going, so there was a quick crack of the whip and Jacko and me were back to work. Being winter it wasn't long before the light faded and the afternoon drew to an early close and Jacko and I were off to get ready for the evening's soiree.

As we headed north I mused on the thought of putting a heavy rock band on stage in a venue such as Trentham Gardens. Set in 1000 acres of woodlands and beautiful gardens, originally designed by Capability Brown, Trentham Hall is the ancestral home of the Duke of Sutherland. Built in 1633, it was largely rebuilt in the eighteenth century and then later remodelled in the nineteenth. The band was to appear in the Grand Hall, which is a large ballroom with a first floor balcony, which neatly contained a bar for the band's guests. So tonight, a Zeppelin would buzz this regal home. Would it still be standing in the morning?

Upon our arrival at the hall a hundred or so fans were already milling around. Heading for the bar we found a space, settled, and waited for Led Zeppelin to arrive on stage. The buzz of anticipation was audible by the time the hall was half full, and for any of you that were there, Jacko was the one in the suit. I can't recall now if they started on time, though I doubt it. Eventually the house lights dimmed, John kick-started the kit into life, making it sound like a pneumatic hammer was pounding the snare. Jacko and I stood watching proudly as the boys yet again gave their all in a show that melded talent with sheer magic. Some 20 years on, whilst writing his book 'Underground Tapes', Luis Ray wrote of the show, "Released on two CDs, 'Stoke Volumes 1 & 2', this is the finest document for enjoying Bonzo's drumming at its most careful and precise."

As members of the family gathered to discuss what a great night it had been, somewhere in the distance an angry exchange could be heard. Although the bar hall had emptied of people, it hadn't emptied of smoke, so it was difficult to see what was going on. We could only go by voice recognition – and yes, our ears had not let us down, it was our John, and he was going totally apeshit. Suddenly it went quiet and as the smoke cleared, we could see that John had disappeared, so assorted members of the band's entourage set off in various directions in order to locate the missing drummer.

John was nowhere to be found, so it was back to the bar to figure out what to do next. Our thoughts were soon interrupted by a huge cry of "What the fuck was that?" echoing across the hall. It was in response to a loud crashing sound from somewhere outside the hall and everyone headed towards the exit door. Now, I think it's time I should let you know about the parking arrangements that had been made for the band. John had driven to the gig in his Rolls Royce, so for protection it was decided it would be best parked in an enclosed courtyard, which had large wooden doors to secure it. Well that's what the loud bang had been. John had stormed out of the building, jumped into his motor and driven it straight through the large doors while they were still closed, leaving a passable impression of a large mousehole behind him.

It was at this point that the evening descended into some kind of sub-Wacky Races farce, as everyone jumped into their cars and set off after John 'Dick Dastardly' Bonham. It's a real shame I don't have any photographs of this night, but the following should give you some sort of idea.

John's attire for the evening had been a very loud check suit and the largest rainbow coloured bow tie you have ever seen. So here's the picture: we're looking for a young rock drummer with long hair, a heavy beard and is dressed like Coco the Clown, driving a Rolls Royce at high speed down the M6 motorway on his way home. Except we're heading one way down the M6 south and John, who has joined the Motorway by the wrong slip road is heading North to Scotland.

We later found out that he realised what he'd done when he saw a sign for Liverpool so he'd taken another slip road and managed to get off the motorway. However, before he could turn back he needed to find a garage for his gas-guzzler.

Sadly, it was too late, and as he headed towards Liverpool the heart-sinking sound of an engine running out of fuel was heard. 'Bollocks' is the only word I can imagine John to have said as the car spluttered to a halt. Now it's Sod's Law that a car without petrol will always end up at the farthest point possible from a garage, and tonight was no exception.

The cold dark night was none too inviting, but this was the era well before mobile phones so John had little choice. Luckily he hadn't been walking too far when he saw a wagon parked up in a lay-by. Even better, a light was on behind the curtains, which hopefully meant the driver was still awake. John's pace quickened until he was stood below the driver's door. Reaching up, he knocked on the window and waited. As the curtains parted, John could see the face of a man who looked like he shaved with broken bottles and wiped his arse with hedgehogs – you know, the 'happy-go-lucky truckie'. Undaunted, John stood his ground and was still standing there as the truck disappeared down the road. It turned out that the driver was not as tough as he appeared. He took one look at the nutter stood outside his lorry, fired up the engine and got the hell out of there.

Eventually, having walked further down the road, John found a phone box and called home. The ever-faithful

Matthew set off, post-haste, up the M6 to retrieve the missing drummer. It wasn't the first time during the five years he had worked for John that he'd had to leave his bed in the early hours to go looking for him. It wasn't the last either.

The next morning Jacko and I swapped our guest list garb for woolly hats and welly boots and got on with the job in hand. We didn't see John that day, but as you can imagine we weren't allowed to laugh about this for sometime (well, only behind closed doors). We kept our heads down for the next few days and if John popped in, well, nothing was mentioned about our night out.

We never did find out what upset him.

Chapter 15

THE ELUSIVE MOBY DICK

It was during the time we spent building 'The Old Hyde' that John regained his love of fishing, so on several occasions he would arrive on site to see if Matt and I fancied a day's sport on the riverbank. "Bloody right", would be the reply, because no matter how bad the fishing was, it always beat working. Don't get me wrong, I loved working on the farm, but a rod in one hand and a beer in the other feels a lot better than a shovel in one hand and a blister on the other. These trips would only happen about once a year, mainly because we were so bad at it. After watching a float do bugger all throughout the day, it would be at least a year before anyone fancied going near the river for a while.

Late in the summer of 1973, John was recuperating after a gruelling 36-date tour of America and arrived on the farm seeking fishing partners for the next day. Of course Matt and I were up for it, so we spent the rest of the afternoon planning a fishing trip. Matt delved into the darkest recesses of the garage to find John's fishing tackle, while I was despatched off to the tackle shop to pick up a variety of baits to entice the fish. Most of the evening was spent hunting around at home in search of my thermos flask and preparing sandwiches for the big day.

The alarm clock exploded on the bedside table at the unearthly hour of 3.30am – time to be river bound. We'd arranged to meet at 4.30am in the car park near where John's boat was moored. When I arrived it was still dark but morning was slowly breaking in the distance, lending an eerie silhouette to the roofs and chimney pots of the old town of Stourport on the other side of the river. John and Matthew arrived shortly afterwards and, gear in hand; we made our way to the boat.

Straws would be drawn to see who fished where and to my delight, I was to fish off the boat, while John and

Matt fished off the bank. John seemed none too impressed with this but it was too late as I was already on the boat sorting out my armchair. As I set my rod up I realised why I loved fishing so much. Dawn's early light catching the mist rising off the river was a sight to behold and the fish were beginning to jump to catch flies and feeding on other morsels floating downstream. On a morning like this it would soothe even the most savage beast, and it was going to need to by the time we were finished.

I whistled loudly to signify the match was underway. Honour was at stake and a lot of money was on for who would win the day. The usual stakes applied – £1 for the biggest fish, £1 for the most fish and £1 for over-all weight. Sometimes one catch would snare all three prizes. Time dragged at snail's pace; by 7.00am not a fish had been landed, nor had anyone even had a bite. It was times like these that I wondered who had come first, the Three Stooges, or us. Then, like a bolt out of the blue John was up, cutting the morning air like Zorro. The trouble was that when John's float had dipped under the water he'd used a little too much power to hook the fish, thus catapulting the small fish into the next field and his float and hook into the top of a tree. By now I was having to bite a hole in my lip to stop myself from laughing 'cos knowing John I would have ended up at the top of the same tree. Thankfully I remembered that there was a café nearby so I beat a hasty retreat to get some bacon sarnies for everyone. When I got back John had sorted his problem and was fishing again, but I could tell from the look on his face that the last 15 minutes had well pissed him off. Shortly after the sandwiches, John said he was off to the café to use the loo, and if things hadn't got any better by the time he came back we might as well pack up and go back to work.

Matthew and I stood there like two kids who'd just been told Christmas had been cancelled and what made it worse was that we had about a quarter of an hour to come up with an idea, which for us was about as rare as rocking-horse shit. Still, what we came up with was this; we tied my line to John's line and waited for him to come back. As he appeared I gave my line a sharp tug, making it look like he'd hooked a big fish. At this John dived down the riverbank, grabbing the rod. Of course, there was no fish, but he was encouraged to stay a little longer. Luckily for Matt and I, the fishing did improve, so much so that John won the competition.

John's fishing career took its final blow when we were invited by a friend of ours to accompany him to a pool where he claimed we would "catch a lot of big fish". I do believe anyone stupid enough to make such a claim should be named, and as this story shows, a certain chap named Mick Lanfear should not be listened to.

We arrived at the pool, which was by the side of the River Severn a few miles south of Worcester. After paying our fees, we set out to find a good spot to fish from. John picked out what he thought was a good 'swim' and Mick and I went further around the pool.

The two of us started catching fish quite soon, but after a couple of hours John hadn't moved and didn't look best pleased. We couldn't understand why he wasn't catching fish but it didn't really matter because he stood up, slowly and neatly packed away all his tackle and then threw the lot into the middle of the pool. As we sat watching the basket sink through tears of laughter in our eyes, John kicked a large piece of meat into the water. Stunned, we sat and watched a bloody big pike swim out from under the landing stage John had been sat on and gulped the lot down. Now we knew why there were no big fish. That sorted and smelling like a shithouse door made of fish boxes, we set off for the pub to drown our sorrows. Moby Dick would live to fight another day.

It wasn't until some years later, when I took my young son James with me on a fishing trip, that he said we should call it rodding, because fish didn't enter the equation. From the mouths of babes, I realised I was one shit fisherman.

BONZO ON TOURING

"There are some bands who tour America as many times as possible, but although we could do this, the result would be that the audience would go along for the sake of going to a concert and not because it's an event. Before long your prestige goes and you burn yourself out. You must create your own demand."

"Sometimes touring gets a bit wearing, but that's only because I'm married with kids at home. I've never gotten pissed off with the actual touring. I enjoy playing – I could play every night. It's just being away that gets you down sometimes. I still enjoy going through different towns that we haven't been to before. But you get fed up with places like New York because they're not interesting anymore."

On touring in the USA:
"The restaurant scene in the South can be unbelievable. We've stopped for a coffee and watched everybody in the place get service. People who came in after we did. Everybody sits and glares at you, waiting and hoping that you'll explode and start a scene."

On touring in the USA:
"We even had a gun pulled on us in Texas. Some guy was shouting out and giving us general crap about our hair and all: we simply gave it back to him. We were leaving after the show and this same guy turned up at the door. He pulls out this pistol and says to us, 'You guys gonna do any shouting now?' We cleared out of there *tout de suite.*"

"We enjoy playing. Every gig is important to us. In this business, it doesn't matter how big you are, you can't afford to become complacent. If you adopt that attitude, you're dead. That'll never happen to us."

119

Chapter 16

DOWN ON THE FARM

Towards the end of 1972, Brian Treble, a young man from Lincolnshire, had come through an interview with flying colours and had become the new farm manager at Old Hyde. Brian and his young wife Lin had moved into the newly renovated cottage and were hard at work putting the farm back together. The main order for Brian was to eventually breed Hereford cattle and produce the Rushock Herd of Pedigree Hereford Cattle. Brian worked with such enthusiasm that it didn't take him long to have the Old Hyde ticking over like a working farm should.

With work on the house going well to plan, John went back to work with Jimmy, Robert and John Paul and on 3 March began their third European tour. On the French leg of the tour an Atlantic Records employee, Benoit Gautier, joined them. After spending a couple of days with the band, he would remark that Led Zeppelin looked, "like the cast of Robin Hood, being played by the inmates from an asylum!" He had also noted that when Bonzo was drunk, he would often groan, and thus referred to him as 'Le Bete', or The Beast.

John made a couple of flying visits to the farm during April, before going on to rehearsals at Shepperton Studios, readying themselves for the biggest tour of the States Zeppelin had yet undertaken. Between 4 May and 29 July the band would pass through 33 cities, playing to audiences larger than anyone could have imagined. On the opening night of the tour, 49,000 people crowded into the Braves Stadium in Atlanta. That was topped the very next day at Tampa Stadium, Florida, when Led Zeppelin would enter into the *Guinness Book of Records* having played to an audience of 56,800, the largest attendance (at the time) for a single performance in history, which netted the band over $309,000. With the large amounts of money rolling in – the tour grossed

Above
John Bonham, Peter Grant, Jimmy Page
and John Paul Jones

$4.5 million and *The Financial Times* reported in May of that year that Led Zeppelin had grossed $30 million that year – Peter hired *The Starship* to fly the Zep entourage around America. The plane was a Boeing 720B converted into a flying hotel, with bedrooms, bar and innumerable other luxuries. It was just marvellous for having parties whilst flying to gigs.

The tour culminated in three nights at Madison Square Garden, where the band shot live footage for a film they were planning. During his stay at the Drake Hotel in New York, someone did a runner with $200,000 of the band's money, which was supposedly stolen out of the hotel's safety deposit box. The group returned home and would not gig again until January 1975.

Down on the farm everything was running to plan. The house was well underway and Brian had accrued a small herd of Hereford cows and one frisky bull called Bruno, whose job it was to just saunter around the field occasionally awarding the 'ladies' a portion.

After a couple of weeks' rest, John arrived at the farm, this time closely followed by a complete film crew. They were there to film John's fantasy sequence for the forthcoming film *The Song Remains the Same*, but to John it was no fantasy. He just wanted to do what he enjoyed the most, which was being on the farm with his family, playing a game of snooker down the local Conservative Club, racing fast cars and having a pint down his local. The film would include two of his latest acquisitions; a Model T Ford Ice Truck that had been turned into a work of art, and a chopper bike built in America but with a British-built 650cc Bonneville engine. Instant T, as the rod was called, had won the Oklahoma Custom Car Show and was powered by a 7-litre engine with a 'blower' which would propel the vehicle up to 60mph in just under 3 seconds. The bike was no slouch either, as John and Mathew found out as they left The New Inn. Too many revs had been applied, as John kicked the bike into gear, and he was sent flying straight across the road and through the hedge. Fortunately this was not caught on film.

During a sequence filmed in Blackpool the local police had to be informed of what was going on. Their only stipulation was that John had to wear a crash helmet, which tended to spoil the desired shot. The finale, you see, would feature John powering down Santa Pod drag strip in Clive Skilton's AA Fueler, a segment with some of the best editing I have ever seen, when the engine is firing in time with John's drum solo.

The other form of transport seen in the film was a horse and cart, which is used to take John and Pat out on a country ride, but the horse in question, Old Sam, could only make it to the front gate and back again. Sam had been sold to John as a young horse in his prime but doubts were soon aired when John had hitched him up and travelled on him to the local pub about a mile away. A horsebox had to be dispatched to pick Sam up because he was totally knackered. When the vet was called out to examine him he reckoned he was old enough to have led the Charge Of The Light Brigade. Another clue to his true age was that every morning when we arrived for work he would be lying flat out in his field, sound asleep, and would not rise until after 10.00am.

Although Led Zeppelin was not touring, the band kept busy with several projects. Recording of their next album, 'Physical Graffiti', was underway at Headley Grange, and they were also setting up their own record label, Swan Song. Acts signed to this label included Bad Company, featuring Paul Rodgers, Boz Burrell, Simon Kirke and Mick Ralphs, The Pretty Things and Maggie Bell. Swan Song was to be run from offices in the Kings Road, Chelsea, ironically situated across from The World's End pub, and the label was launched with big parties in New York and Los Angeles.

As all this tooing and froing was going on, all Brian's hard work and sleepless nights had paid off. A healthy bull calf had been born, much to the excitement of everybody working on the farm. As a celebration, we invited Brian over to the Conservative Club along with Pete and Stan, to wet the baby's head, and although Brian didn't drink he was so chuffed about the calf he came over just to be with his workmates. As the night progressed Brian was looking tired so he left early to go to bed. Nothing could have prepared us for the news we received the next morning. As Jacko and I were getting ready to go to work we received a phone call saying that Brian had been killed in a road accident on his way home from the club. Everyone was devastated, as Brian had become such an integral part of the project with his enthusiasm and hard work. The added tragedy was that he had left his young wife Lin expecting their first child.

The news of Brian's death had upset John immensely, and he didn't want anyone else running the farm, so for a short while Mathew and I took over. Our first problem was that we knew nothing about farming, but the local farming community all rallied around to help. One man who would be an incredible asset to us was a chap called Am. Of Italian descent, Am owned a farm a couple of miles away and would come down every morning to show us what to do and then go back to his own farm. Another major problem was that it was the start of the lambing season, Mathew and I camped in the unfinished house so we could keep an eye on the sheep throughout the night. If we spotted a ewe in trouble we had to go and help with the birth. The only trouble with this for me is that I'm what you might call a bit squeamish, so when it came to a hands on situation, I just pulled my hat down and followed Matt's instructions. After two solid weeks on the farm, 24-hours a day I was awarded a day off. Upon my return the following day I found an irate Bonzo fuming because I was a bit late. A few short, sharp exchanges later and I was fired. Again!

Clad in Donkey jacket, jeans and wellies, I strode off down the drive and headed home in the knowledge that someone would come and pick me up and take me back to work. Four miles down the road this idea seemed to be wearing a little thin, but the next day there was John on the phone asking why I wasn't at work and laughing about the events of the previous day.

"We were doing some dates in Texas and Bonzo and I ended up in a rather rough looking bar," John Paul Jones

recalls, of an incident which sheds much light on John's fondness for life back home on the farm. "Bonzo was in high spirits so I was trying to keep a low profile behind him. As we made our way through the bar the place went quiet and everybody's interest seemed focused on us. A few long hair clichés were aimed at us, so Bonzo started to give as good as he got. At this I wanted to get out of the place but Bonzo ordered more drinks. The atmosphere was turning nasty and it looked like we might end up in trouble, but as only Bonzo could, he turned and asked 'Okay, what sort of cattle do you boys raise around here?' The whole atmosphere changed and within minutes everyone had gathered round and were talking about Longhorns and Steers and there in the middle was Bonzo talking about his Herefords and what feeds were the best. He had this amazing knack of getting out of sticky situations and could talk his way out of anything."

Returning back to work, we finally finished off the house towards the end of 1974. There was some good news for Swan Song as well at this time, as Bad Company's self-titled debut album had hit the Number One slot in the States.

Eventually a new manager did take over at the farm, but it would never seem the same again. And with the completion of the house came the completion of my work, so for me it was on the road again. The last two years had been a lot of fun, working with Jacko and John and hearing about the progress of the band first-hand from stories that John told us. Now it was back to the real world of following the band through the music papers.

Chapter 17

MAY DAZE

"Bonham's solo: it's a tight, densely-packed cross-weave of intersecting rhythms which includes an astounding number of variations without ever losing its basic beat. It just keeps on coming, and it's cohesive enough to stand up as a piece of music, and simultaneously varied enough to keep the listener from nodding out. Many light years away it is from the usual random collection of redundant percussion exercises.

It goes into three sections: drums with sticks, drums with hands, and a rather attenuated electronic drum exercise before a return to the main theme with the sticks."

Charles Shaar Murray's, review of Zeppelin at Earls Court 1975

On 11 January 1975, Led Zeppelin would finally perform as a band again in Rotterdam, their first gigs since July '73. With another gig the following night in Brussels, these two dates would act as a warm up for their forthcoming American tour. As it was with most of the previous tours of the States, the sceptics were busy saying that Zep couldn't do it again and wouldn't do as well this time. And yet again they were proved wrong when all 700,000 concert tickets had been sold before they arrived for their first show in Minneapolis on 18 January. This tour would see them perform 37 shows with an entourage of 44 and three large truck loads of equipment, which included a 70,000 watt PA system and a 310,000 watt lighting rig.

Tickets had been in such demand that rioting had occurred at many venues, the worst of which was at The Boston Garden, resulting in the band being banned from appearing there. After a short break in March they carried on through Texas, ending the tour with three nights at The Forum in Los Angeles. Here John bought another car for his collection, a Ford Sedan built to hot

The Graffiti
of the Physical...

rod specifications, and decided to try it out racing up and down Sunset Trip.

"He had just bought this new motor and was doing about 90mph up and down the strip," recalls John Paul Jones. "He was going mad, and you know what the police are like over there about speeding. Anyway, it wasn't long before the Highway Patrol pulled him over and they jump out of the car, with guns already out. At this, John jumps out of his car shouting 'Hold on, hold on!' One of the officers briskly asked John, 'What the fuck do you think you're doing?' to which he replied, 'Well look, I've just come back from The Forum where we just played a blinding gig and I've got this brand new car'. And then he says, 'Come and have a look at it' and opens the bonnet. The cops are looking at him and he says, 'Come on, come and have a look at this. You have a look at the bloody size of the engine'. I'm watching all this from the Hyatt House Hotel and it's gone from an emergency situation to them all looking under the hood discussing brake horsepower. The next thing the police are leaving telling Bonzo to go steady next time and him offering them tickets for the next show. It was amazing, but he got away with it again."

During the latter half of the tour, Led Zeppelin's sixth album, 'Physical Graffiti' had been released in America and had already shifted one million in advance orders. It went on to top the charts around the world and they became the first rock band to have all their albums in the Billboard Top 200 at the same time.

Also during January, on the other side of the Atlantic, Lin and I were discussing some important dates of our own. We had been together for six years and we decided to get married on 13 September and were busy arranging everything; the church, reception and honeymoon. Since finishing work at Old Hyde I had hardly seen John, so on Jacko's birthday, John and Mathew came over and we took Jacko out on a pub-crawl. As the night wore on John told us about the gigs they were due to do at Earls Court in London, and that extra nights had been added due to ticket demand. As we left the Conservative Club a little after 1.00am, John gave us some tickets for the show on 23 May before Matt took him home and Jacko and I wobbled back to the flat.

It seems crazy that in some of the previous years Led Zeppelin could hardly get any media coverage in this country, and yet now, with the build up to the Earls Court dates, every paper was carrying articles about them. Even *The Observer*!

Come 23 May Jacko, Debbie and myself, along with a good friend of mine, Roger Haymes, set off to see for ourselves how the band had progressed since we had last seen them at Trentham Gardens. As soon as the band walked on stage, to rapturous applause, we were in awe. Showco had shipped in the PA system and light show that was used on their American tour, and above the stage was a huge video screen showing close up views of the band as they went about their business. For three and a half hours we were treated to rock music from a band that you just knew were glad to be home. Every enthusiastic move by the band was highlighted in a show that was second to none. Laser beams fired above the heads of the audience gave the effect of flaming arrows when they reflected off a mirror ball, filling the vast hall with snowflakes and stars, You didn't need chemicals that night to scorch your brain.

While John was in full flight during 'Moby Dick', Jacko was up and dancing in the aisles with the best of them. And as everyone looked on quizzically at this older person in a suit he just kept telling everyone, "That's my boy". As I watched Jacko watching John I realised that there's nothing more contented than the face of a father watching a son (or daughter) achieve their ambitions.

After the show we were to meet up with John and the other members of the band backstage for a drink. A large caravan had been towed in to act as a dressing room and drinks dispensary, so we knew where we were headed. As we arrived John came over and hugged everybody, asking us what we wanted to drink. A crew member disappeared into the van for the drinks. Beers for us, of course, but only coke for little Debbie. I had to laugh when I heard a voice in the van shout, "Not that you fucking idiot, it's for John's little sister. Coca Cola stupid!"

About two weeks later, on 10 June, Pat gave birth to a baby girl called Zoe. John phoned us to tell us the news and arranged to come over to the Conservative Club to celebrate that night. Jacko and I arrived at 8.00pm and waited for John. By 9.00pm there was still no sign of him so we carried on with our own celebration. At 10.30pm the stewardess came over to say that John was on the phone. It appeared that he had popped in at The New Inn for a quick one but it had ended up a party and he wanted Jacko and me to pop over. There was no way we could go as neither of us were in a fit state to drive and at that time there were no garages open to even get petrol.

At 11.15pm John rang again, this time in a terrible temper, and gave me a real bollocking for not going over, but as I tried to explain what the problem was the phone went dead. Jacko and I headed home, but shortly after midnight a heavy battering at the door told me John had arrived. As I opened the door he burst in and tried to knock the crap out of me, with Jacko trying to get between us and stop the pandemonium. In the ensuing tussle Jacko took a knock, which cut his lip. At this, John stopped, hugged his dad and apologised. He then turned to me and said, "Look what you've done now", aiming a few more blows in my direction, before he stopped again having noticed the décor. Jacko had been given some paint and had decided to paint the lounge. The only problem was that Jacko was colour-blind and nobody had told him that the paint was lime green and orange. John looked around the room in disbelief, which gave me a breather, then again focused on the job in hand, shouted at me again, then disappeared out the door.

Although we'd had several good scraps with each other whilst growing up, this would be different. It would be almost a year before John and I made contact with each other. No matter what happened though, I would still follow his career through news articles in various papers, while John spent the next 12 months away from his family, an exile from England.

Chapter 18

CELEBRATION DAY

On Saturday 13 September, I woke early and looked out at the world through bloodshot eyes. A stag night that had lasted all week had certainly taken its toll and today of all days I wanted to enjoy every minute, because within a few hours I would marry the beautiful girl who had been with me for the last six years. I had met Lin back in 1969, at about the same time John went off with Zeppelin and she had been with me through all the ups and downs, and had stayed with me. Being so eager not to be late, my best man, Spencer Chapman, managed to get me to the church an hour early. The only thing to do was to have a quick hair of the dog over at the Unicorn Hotel, before taking the plunge. Quite fitting really, as Jacko had also had a drink in the Unicorn before taking the plunge; out of the window on VE night many years before. So, with nerves calmed, we made our way back to St. Stephens Church, near the town centre.

At 1.30pm, escorted by her father Stanley and followed by the bridesmaids, Rosita, Julie and my younger sister Debbie, Lin joined me at the altar, as we became husband and wife. Along with the birth of my two children, it would be one of the three happiest days of my life, and as we said our vows and then danced the night away, I would occasionally glance out of the window in the hope that I may see John arrive, but alas, it was not to be. Sadly, I had always believed that on my own wedding day my big brother would have been by my side.

Prior to the wedding, Lin and I had managed to acquire a two bedroomed flat, so on our return from honeymoon we started our new life at 11 Dolben Lane, Winyates. Situated on the top floor of a three-storey building, with glass patio doors in the lounge, one could just sit and look over one's 'estate'. It was here that I would ponder just what it was that had caused such an upheaval between John and myself, and it all seemed to boil down to a misunderstanding when the wedding plans had been made at the beginning of the year. We had already booked our wedding when John told us that Pat's brother Jeff had also booked his wedding on the same day and was there any chance of us changing our date. At this late stage it would have been an impossible task, and I'm sure this mix up had a lot to do with what happened on the night of baby Zoe's birth. It wouldn't be for many years that I would find out just how much it had actually hurt John not to be at our wedding, something I would never have wanted to happen.

But now as a married man I needed to put food on the table, so in the post Old Hyde search for employment, I had taken on full-time work at Dollydisc. Dollydisc was, if you can contain your laughter, an all-female, disco dancing, music playing, go anywhere, drinking disco outfit. It consisted of five girls; Connie Chapman would play the music while Karen Pennington, Jilly Davies, Vicky Harten and Annie would do all the drinking and dancing. All the equipment had been designed and built by Connie's husband, Spencer who had been a designer of some acclaim at the BBC, and it was our job to get the equipment and the girls in working order at venues around the country. It was as we travelled around the country in a little, old Bedford van that memories of the early band days in the 60s came flooding back, only instead of five guys having a whip round for petrol we had five girls having a whip round for a bottle of wine. The majority of our work came from the British and American Air Force bases, where we would perform on the Officer's Mess. I'd love to know where that name comes from, because these places really were the dog's bollocks, you know. I'm talking Five star hotel stuff and we were treated in style. So when we were invited to appear at the Sergeants Mess at a Royal Air Force base (which will remain nameless as I don't want to contravene the Official Secrets Act) we never expected to be playing in what appeared to be a big shed situated between two runways. But against all odds the evening went very well, until some kind soul gave permission for an aircraft to take off without informing us. At first we thought it was thunder until the whole building started to shake, scaring the shit out of all of us.

Still, these bases treated us well and we always had a good time, but if you really wanted to party, it had to be one of the American bases. These guys were in charge of the Early Warning System, which could track down a fart in a Force 9 gale, and I was to make friends with many of the lads, but one in particular, called Joe, would always look after us whenever we were there. It was Joe who introduced me to the Double 7, which was a large measure of *Seagrams VO7* topped up with *Seven Up*, and by the end of the night he didn't know where he was, let alone the enemy. Indeed, it led me to believe that if they were looking after us, who the hell looks after them?

Eventually, mileage would take its toll so Connie and Spence, purchased a beautiful old country house, where they planned to open their own club and bring audiences to them. The name of the place was Ettington Park Manor and it stood in its own grounds some six miles south of Stratford-upon-Avon, and gave it the appearance of a stately home that could have doubled for the set of *The Munsters*. With its eerie presence and its own small church set at the side, it had been used as the set for the classic horror film *The Haunting* (the 60s original mind you, and not the dire 90s remake). Still, whenever I stayed there I always slept with the light on.

Turning Ettington into a club would take a lot of hard work and a lot of hard cash, so it had to be a working venue and, once a couple of rooms were finished, it was opened to the public. During the day Spence and I would do all the renovating while Connie, Jill and Karen did the administration. Come night time, we would be barmen and the girls would return to being Dollydisc.

During one of my rare weekends off, Lin and I were relaxing in the lounge, watching the world go by from our balcony perch when in the distance came the sound of a very powerful motor car coming our way. Lin gave me a quizzical look and said, "That's John." It couldn't be I said, as the music papers had said he'd had to go and live abroad. Still the sound drew nearer and we looked out to see who it was. The car that pulled into the car park was the sort of thing you'd imagine either John or

Cruella DeVill owning, but without waiting to find out I was up and running down the three flights of stairs and out into the car park to find John walking towards me with that heart-warming smile across his face. No words were exchanged, we just hugged each other until Lin arrived and joined in. We made our way back to the flat, all babbling away at once and inside John told us over the next few hours about everything that had been happening; about Robert and Maureen's bad crash, that the film would be out in 1976 and about work on the new album 'Presence'. He also told us about his hatred of having to live away from his family, and was only allowed so many days back in the country and that he would have to leave again tomorrow.

One thing he did want to know about was how was Jacko. Immediately memories of that fateful night returned, but John just burst out laughing and said, "I couldn't ask at the time, but what had Jacko done to his lounge?" What he was referring to was how Jacko had decorated the room, so I told him the story of how he'd been working on a job and discovered several tins of discarded paint. Thinking he could save a few bob, he'd brought them home and painted the lounge. This was all okay for Jacko because he was totally colour-blind, but you could see why no one had wanted the paint. Jacko had ended up with three very bright orange walls and one lime green one. To Jacko it looked great but to the unsuspecting guest it merely had the effect of snow blindness. By the time I'd finished explaining we both had tears running down our faces, visualising a whistling Jacko painting away. John left for Coventry the next day and I returned to work at the Manor a very contented man.

'John had spent his year of non-residency in hotel rooms in New York, Jersey and the south of France, fighting off boredom and other people.'

John had spent his year of non-residency in hotel rooms in New York, Jersey and the south of France, fighting off boredom and other people. Originally a world tour had been booked to coincide with the time the band would be away from England. That had to be shelved after Robert's tragic car accident, and with no gigs the year dragged on for what seemed like an eternity. One break in the monotony came when the band were in Montreaux, at the same time as the Jazz Festival. John

Paul Jones had talked John into going to see the Count Basie Orchestra. While watching the show John had become interested in the drummer and Jonesy asked if he'd like to meet him. John became apprehensive, asking why Basie's drummer would want to meet him, but backstage the roles were reversed. It turned out that the drummer was one of John's biggest fans and had studied his style and copied a lot of his techniques. That meant a lot to a drummer in a Rock'n'Roll band.

Still, during the band's exile the fans had not forgotten about Led Zeppelin and in both the *Melody Maker* and *New Musical Express* polls, Zeppelin took eight awards. Although it was a great achievement for the band, that elusive Number One drummer slot still eluded John. Making up for that somewhat was the news that the band's new album 'Presence' had already gone platinum in America, on advance orders alone.

Arriving back home in May 1976, we all met up at the Conservative Club in Studley and, although it had been a year since our last night out, I was glad to see that silliness was still the order of the day. What still amazed me was that John could still get away with it, even at the Club. While playing a frame of snooker, John hit the cue ball so hard that it left the table and demolished one of the wall lights. His punishment? Cries of "Good shot John" from the other members watching the game. Now if I had done that the committee would have held an emergency meeting and a suitable candidate would have been chosen to kick my arse out the door.

During the time I hadn't seen John, his now 10-year old son Jason had become involved in Schoolboy Moto Cross, and with immense help from Pat's brother-in-law Allan, had started racing at local meetings. While John was away Allan would become a one-man pit stop, doing all the mechanics, being transport and making sure Jason was alright. Lin and I finally saw him race in June '76, and although I thought that cowboys and indians would be a much safer bet, Jason wasn't scared and became a very competent rider. Soon the whole Schoolboy thing would become a big part of John's life too.

'Still, during the band's exile the fans had not forgotten about Led Zeppelin and in both the Melody Maker and New Musical Express polls, Zeppelin took eight awards.'

139

Above
Jason Bonham

Chapter 19

BIRTHS AND PREMIERES

While John had gone back to America to be at the premiere of the new film *The Song Remains the Same* in New York, then a few days later in Los Angeles, I was at home trying to console a wife with a rather large bump where her slim stomach had once been. On 30 October I began to suss out that something odd was about to happen when I was sent to the shops on two occasions, firstly for chocolate and then tinned pears. Upon my return with the pears I found that Lin's mum and dad had called in for coffee. Lin arrived in the kitchen and announced that her waters had broken. This is where all the studying on the subject really helped as I shouted, "Shit, don't tell me, tell your mum!"

I was immediately sent back to the shopping centre to find a phone box and inform the hospital that we were on our way. I had left the house in such a panic that it wasn't until I felt my feet getting wet in a puddle of God knows what, that I realised that I'd left the house with no shoes on. As I rushed back to the flat, carefully side-stepping the multitude of sharp objects strewn around the place, I repeated that happy mantra "Ooh, ah, shit" over and over again.

The night was spent sat with other, rapidly ageing expectant fathers, and it really didn't look like there'd be enough cigarettes to last until morning. Amidst all this chaos a nurse entered the room and said that Lin was having a bad time and calling for me. Early on in the pregnancy it was decided that I wouldn't attend the birth because I was the bloke who covered his eyes when Bambi's mother got shot, but it was too late now. As I sat there holding Lin's hand, staring into her eyes, she took great pleasure in systematically crushing every finger I possessed. The pain soon disappeared as Emma Michelle coughed and spluttered into life.

After making several phone calls informing the new grandparents, I went over to tell John and Pat the good news. Celebrations were held in the best possible taste, with the consumption of a couple of bottles of the old Dom Perignon, while I spoke incessantly about the previous night's events. With the excitement still buzzing through me I returned to the hospital to be with Lin and Emma. The celebrations would carry on later that evening, at The Green Dragon in Sambourne, along with Jacko and two close friends, Alan and Sue Pitt. At 8.30pm the party got underway and grew louder as the night wore on, terminating with John and I passing out at the same time and being driven home. Lin and our little girl arrived home on 6 November.

On 4 November the UK premiere of *The Song Remains the Same* ran concurrently at the Warner West End cinema and the ABC in Shaftsbury Avenue. A little over two weeks later, on the 21st, it would be premiered in Birmingham at the Futurist Cinema in the centre of town. The evening would begin at Old Hyde with a gathering of friends and family, while we waited for the coach that had been laid on to take us to the cinema. As we had a couple of drinks at the house, John looked rather nervous and then he told me he was a little worried how people would take to the film.

Nerves soon started to disappear when everyone had arrived and we set off for Brum in the old charabanc (good old name for a coach in Brum and pronounced 'sharabong' in the Black Country accent. Don't forget, up here 'bonk' isn't sex, it's what you sit on when you're fishing).

The film had met with a very mixed reaction from the critics. Some loved it, some hated it but I LOVED it. I had waited a long time to see John's sequence after all the hard work that had been put into it. I also wanted to see the parts that I had been involved with and maybe, just maybe, I might be spotted by a director and end up in films. Come the end of the movie I realised that the only person who would spot me would be the chap who empties the bins in the editing suite. Shit, even Old Sam the horse had got his face in.

Above
Melody Maker Awards. John Bonham and
Jimmy Page with band members from Camel
and Uriah Heep receiving their awards

Opposite
Bonham and Page with Billy Connolly
centre, the only person to interview John
live on TV. (The interview lasted two
minutes!)

After the premiere a reception for all the guests had been arranged at The Opposite Lock, a nightclub at the side of the canal by Gas Street. Whilst everyone ate the vol-au-vents and discussed the film, a DJ took his position and the party really started. After a while young Jason spotted a drum kit on the stage so he got up and played along with the records. As a young drummer he was having the time of his life and the audience responded with rapturous applause. But, and you just knew there'd be a but, the DJ said something about Jason's drumming and said "Play this…" putting Sandy Nelson's 'Let There Be Drums' on. It's a piece of music most drummers would have trouble copying. Not one to refuse a challenge, Jason gave it his best shot, but ended up looking a little embarrassed. The DJ was peering down from his position behind a window above the stage and as we all looked up a large arm appeared in the window, grabbed the DJ around the neck and he disappeared. A little later a loud splash was heard in the canal. Whoops, somebody must have fallen off the 'bonk'. Apart from that small incident the night had been a great success.

Bonzo on the Band

"The whole group gets on well. To me some groups get too close, and the slightest thing can upset the whole band. In this group we're just close enough. It's never a case of somebody saying something and the whole band being on the verge of breaking up.

You get more enjoyment out of playing with each other if you don't know everyone too well. Sometimes it isn't any fun anymore to play with a group you've been in for years, but with Led Zeppelin we're always writing new stuff, doing new things, and every individual is important and getting into new things themselves."

BONZO ON DRUMMING

On playing drums with his hands:

"I can get an absolutely true sound. It hurts at first, but the skin soon hardens and now I can hit a drum harder with my hands than with drum sticks."

"I'd like to have it publicised that I came in *after* Karen Carpenter in the *Playboy* drummer poll! She couldn't last ten minutes with a Zeppelin number"

(Interview 1975)

"I really like to yell out when I'm playing. I yell like a bear to give it a boost. I like our act to be like a thunderstorm. My ambition is to record the 1812 Overture. I would over-dub all the rhythm sections – the bells, cannons and timps. I'll do it one day"

"When I started playing I was most impressed by those early soul records. I like the feel and the sound they achieved. I suppose I said to myself, 'I'll get that sound too.' I've always liked drums to be big and powerful. I've never used cymbals much. I use them to crash into a solo and out of it, but basically I prefer the actual drum sound."

(Interview 1973)

"I never had any lessons. When I first started playing I used to read music. I was very interested in music. But when I started playing in groups I did a silly thing and dropped it. It's great if you can write things down."

(Interview 1973)

"I've always been obsessed with drums. They fascinate me. Any other instrument – nothing. I play acoustic guitar a bit. But it's always been drums first and foremost. I don't reckon on this Jack-of-all-trades thing." "I think that feeling is a lot more important than

technique. It's all very well doing a triple paradiddle – but who's going to know you've done it? If you play technically you sound like everybody else. It's being original that counts."

"I don't consider that I'm particularly influenced by anyone or anything. But when I started playing, I was influenced by early soul. It was just that feel, that sound."

"When I listen to drummers I like to be able to say 'Oh! I haven't heard that before.' Being yourself is so much better than sounding like anyone else. Ginger Baker's thing is that he is himself. So it's no good trying to do what he does."

(1973)

"It's all to do with the swing. You get a much better tone with a big stroke than you do with a short stab."

(1973)

"My son Jason – he plays you know. I've got him a little Japanese drum kit, made to scale. It's got a 14 inch bass drum. He's got his mother's looks, but in character he is just like me. He's always drumming, even when we go out in the car he takes his sticks to bash on the seats. Before the end of Led Zeppelin I'm going to have him on stage with us at the Albert Hall."

(Interview with Chris Welch, June 1975, talking about Moby Dick.)

"I usually play for twenty minutes, and the longest I've ever done was under thirty. It's a long time, but when I'm playing it seems to fly by. There have been times when I have blundered, and got the dreaded look from the lads. But that's a good sign. It shows you're attempting something you've not tried before."

Above
A rare sight. Bonham takes centre stage with,
from left, Max Middleton, Ronne Lane, Keith
Moon, Ray Harper and Jimmy Page,
performing at The Rainbow

Chapter 20

THE CHRISTENING

Emma lay fast asleep in her cot, unaware of all the preparation being made in the other rooms of the flat on her behalf. She was too young to realise that today was 27 February, 1976 and at 4.00pm that afternoon, Emma Michelle Bonham would be christened at St. Peter's Church in the parish of Ipsley.

As Emma slept, Lin and I busied ourselves getting everything ready for all the family and guests, who would return with us after the service for the party to celebrate Emma's christening. Lin was in the kitchen making cakes, trifles and other fancies while I set the bar up in the lounge. As Lin and I occasionally bumped into each other it was apparent that nerves were slowly starting to fray. This was to be the first time since becoming man and wife that we had entertained all of the family at our flat.

Suddenly the sound of food preparation was over-shadowed by the sound of a four-month-old baby crying for her breakfast, and when Emma cried you took notice (something that has never changed to this day). Lin took charge of her while I stocked the fridge with bottles of wine and beer. As zero hour grew nearer it was time for us to get dressed; Emma in a beautiful white christening gown, Lin in her posh frock and me in a suit that looked like it'd had more outings than a Sunday school bus. As we left through the front door to go to the church, both Lin and I glanced back at the flat. Everything was in its place. Lin gave me a look begging assurance that every-thing would go to plan, but in my heart I knew why she was worried. John and I had only seen each other a couple of times since the fight, which had nearly split us up for two years. But we were older now and hopefully wiser, so there was nothing to worry about.

As Lin and I arrived at the church with Emma, all the family and guests had already arrived and were waiting outside. Considering it was February the weather was being kind to us, bathing the church in warm sunlight. St. Peters is a very pretty little church on the outskirts of Redditch, set on top of a hill surrounded by trees. The mild weather had meant that some of the spring flowers were beginning to show through, adding a dash of colour and speciality to the occasion. But as I neared the church, the beauty of the surroundings faded as I saw John and Pat, stood with Jacko, Mum and my little sister Debbie making a family picture that hadn't, for one reason or another, been seen in a while.

Once inside the church Lin and I took our positions by the font and were joined by the chosen godparents. John was to be godfather, while Pat, Lin's sister Rosita and our Debbie were to be godmothers. The service was taken by The Reverend Eeves, which, when you consider that he shared the parish workload with The Reverend Adams, suggested that the Lord's work was certainly being carried out in Redditch.

Water splashed, prayers said, hymns sung and it was time to leave God's house and go back to ours for the party. As the guests arrived at the flat they made their way into the lounge while Lin and I busied ourselves serving refreshments – sherry for the ladies, beer for whoever wanted one. Eventually everyone found a seat and relaxed into conversations regarding the day, which gave me time to have a good chat with John about what was happening with Led Zeppelin and things in general.

Well, so far the day had been a great success, so when it was mentioned that some of the men should adjourn to a local public house to have 'just a quick one', it was agreed to be a good idea. The ladies were left to have a good natter while John, Jacko and I took Allan for a pint. A favourite venue for this kind of excursion was an olde worlde pub called The Green Dragon, a favourite haunt of our grandfather. Set on the side of the village green in the picturesque local village of Sambourne, it was the perfect place for a quiet drink. Once inside you were greeted by the lovely smell of logs burning in an open fire and the broad smile of the friendly landlord Joe

Kimber. Pleasantries exchanged it was time for our 'one pint', and immediately our train came off the rails because Los Trios Bonzos had never been out for only one pint in their lives and tonight was no exception.

One beer led to two, two to four and so on. Time passed unnoticed. I think we were on our sixth when an old acquaintance of ours came into the pub and joined in our conversation. His name was Rene and he owned a hairdressing salon in Studley but was now trying to get into the music management business. The only way to describe Rene, without being rude, would be to say he really rated himself. Now, according to Rene, he had found a band called City Boy and they were apparently going to knock Led Zeppelin off their pedestal. Well, after a couple more beers and another half-hour or so of this verbal assault on John's musical ability my stroppy side reared its ugly head and I went to John's aide, or at least so I thought. But as soon as I went to give this bounder a bit of a slap, John and Jacko went to his aide and began telling me I was out of order. What me, out of order, I thought. That was my first mistake: mixing thinking with drinking because all the brain and mouth could come up with was "well bollocks to the lot of you" and stormed out the door. It was as I left the warm inside and entered the cold outside that the alcoholic boxing glove tried to take my head off and my legs decided that they were going to have nothing to do with me and tried to go another way. Once I had regained control over my legs, I took off in what I thought was the direction home.

"Mick, stop being a prat and come back inside," boomed John's voice into the still, quiet night. Like a flash, my brain had scanned the depths for a reply. "Bollocks," again, was the only thing I could come up with, so now it really was time to get running. I made a quick turn into a dark country lane with John in hot pursuit. After a few minutes, I stopped to catch my breath, but John had swapped shoe leather for car and it had just turned into the lane. I was off like a bullet (well pretty fast for a fat, drunk bloke). Anyway, it was fast enough for me not to notice a garden wall directly in front of me. There wasn't enough time for the brain to get a message to the legs: crash imminent. The thorns ripped into my face as I hurtled earthwards through the rose bush and into the garden beyond.

"Get off my garden or I'll call the police." I looked up to see a very irate lady leaning out of a bedroom window, less than impressed at finding me face down in her garden. I tried to think of a reply, but before I could think, the brain sent the same reply as before. "I beg your pardon? What did you say?" I was just about to tell her again when John's heavy hand landed on the side of my head. As he tried to pull me up I resisted pathetically and both of us ended up face down in the mud. Shouting some grovelling apology to the lady, John bundled me towards the car. I later found out that the lady in question had been the mother of Lin's best friend, Bernie.

As we neared the car Jacko and Allan got out to lend a hand, but as we were all the worse for wear, Jacko ended up hitting his nose on the car door, giving himself a nasty nose bleed. How we drove back to the flat I don't know, but I'll never forget the look on Allan's face. He was not a big drinker, not used to nights like this and he looked very alarmed. Allan Pitt went to live in America shortly after this incident and now lives in Chicago with his second wife Joni and has a nervous twitch in his left eye!

As we entered the flat the room went deathly quiet. All eyes were on us as we stood in the doorway; John caked in mud, Jacko covered in blood and me with blood and mud. Our respective ladies had been particularly gentile during the evening, minding their p's and q's amongst those that didn't drink or swear. But as we stood there "Where the fuck have you been?" resounded around the room in a voice that would shatter glass at 50 paces and suddenly all hell broke loose. Lin started having a real go at me, Pat was giving John a real ear bashing and Mum set about Jacko. Allan was in real shit with his then wife Sue and the poor bloke hadn't done anything. Our Debbie had brought a friend with her from her convent school, Dawn Braithwaite. I remember Dawn, she was a lovely quiet girl from a lovely quiet farming family. The pair of them dived behind the settee until the shouting calmed down. Apparently Dawn still has the lucky 'horse shoe' from the christening cake as a memento of the day she had with 'The Bonham's'.

Whilst everyone was shouting and arguing, John and I sneaked off into the kitchen to find some food. Luckily, there was still some left so we sat down at the table, surrounded by bedlam and got stuck in. Splat! The cake caught me just under the right eye, much to John's amusement, so in retaliation a spoonful of trifle hit him on the chin. By the time Allan's wife Sue walked in, it looked like John had fed me with a catapult. Now for some strange reason, having just given Allan a bollocking, Sue decided to take a liking to me, sitting on my lap and draping her arms around my neck. Maybe it was the cake. Next, in walked Lin, followed by Pat. Much shouting! In walked Debbie and Dawn and began cleaning up and hiding any knives that were on display. Out walked John, trifle on chin saying, "I'm going on bloody tour and I ain't never coming back," and with that he disappeared into the bathroom and locked the door. By the time Lin came down from the ceiling she could see the funny side of things, luckily for me. Strong coffee was made and we went into the lounge to try and calm down.

Heaven knows what time it was when people started to leave, but there was still no sign of John. The toilet door was still locked so I gave it a hefty knock but there was no reply. This called for drastic action so I fetched my toolbox and Jacko set about taking the door off. Suddenly he stopped, turned to me and suggested that it might be a good idea to send the ladies back into the lounge, as no one knew quite what we'd find behind the green door. As the last screw was removed and the door was lifted to one side there was John, bless him, fast asleep on the loo with his trousers round his ankles.

By this time, Debbie and her friend were looking tired, so Dawn got her suitcase and they waited outside the door while Mum said her goodbyes. Although Jacko and

Mum were divorced, with Mum living about 20 miles away in Kidderminster and Jacko in a flat across the road from ours, they had always remained great friends, but I reckon Jacko pushed this friendship to the edge on this particular night. Two minutes after they'd left Debbie came running back saying Jacko had picked up Dawn's suitcase, said "Oh good, we're going on holiday, bacon and eggs," and fallen headfirst into a large bush by the side of the car park. Apparently Mum had said, "Just leave him and get in the car." But Debbie thought better of it and, defying Mum, came to tell us. Poor kid was ever so worried. So, off we went again. We eventually got Jacko into his flat and then returned to ours where John, Pat, Lin and I sat drinking coffee, trying to get John in a fit state to drive. Of course all hope was abandoned and Pat drove back. As we waved them off we glanced back into the flat for the second time that day. This time, it looked like an earthquake zone and took a good two hours to clean up before Lin would let me go to bed.

The next evening we popped over to see Jacko to make sure he was okay. He didn't look too well. He'd not had the most comfortable night's sleep because he'd gone to the loo in the middle of the night, fallen off it and had got himself wedged between the wall and the toilet and that's where he'd spent the night, because the silly old sod had fallen asleep.

I was to see very little of John for the rest of the year, because at the beginning of April Led Zeppelin flew off to America, for their biggest tour to date: 51 shows in 30 cities. More than 1,300,000 fans went to see them during the tour.

What did happen to City Boy?

Chapter 21

OLD FARTS, YOUNG FARTS
(AGE DOESN'T MATTER)

During the time I spent collecting and writing the stories from friends and colleagues, the biggest surprise came when a close friend had bumped into Glenn Matlock from the Sex Pistols. Glenn was the bass player with the band and, although he never achieved the notoriety of say Johnny 'Rotten' Lydon or even his own replacement Sid Vicious, it should be noted that Matlock was the brains behind most of the successful Pistols' songs that still bristle with so much energy and anger, even today.

They say Matlock was booted out of the band for professing a love of the Beatles, ironic really if you recall that post–Pistols, John Lydon, then a member of PIL once wrote to Robert Plant asking him for the lyrics to 'Kashmir', which Lydon wanted to cover. So it seems the influence of old farts was always there with the young farts, if they liked it or not.

Glenn had said that he thought this book was a great idea and, having met John, wished to tell his story. So, a meeting was arranged for me to meet him and find out how Punk and Led Zeppelin ever got together.

The meeting place was to be the Warrington Hotel in Maida Vale, on the up side of London. As I sat there sucking on a Budweiser, waiting for Glenn to arrive, I must admit that I was a little apprehensive meeting a 'Pistol'. How would he look and how would he be dressed? The picture in my mind was a frightening hairstyle with clothes to match. So, when he arrived in very smart, casual clothes and hair groomed to match, the only thing I could think to say was, "Seems we're all a bit older these days". So with that introduction it was decided that we needed more beers and then we could get on with the story.

After 12 months out of the UK and nearly two years since they had played a gig, Led Zeppelin would arrive back in a country that had undergone a dramatic musical change. Punk rock was the order of the day and bands such as the Sex Pistols and The Damned were at the forefront of the assault on the music business.

Glenn Matlock

"We'd all gone down to the Roxy to see The Damned and the place was heaving with people having a good time waiting for the band to come on. Then suddenly the place went quiet and I noticed the whole Led Zeppelin entourage had walked in the door to the welcome of 'What are those old hippies doing here?' and other derogatory remarks, but after a while we thought 'Wait a minute, these are one of the biggest bands in the world and they've bothered to take the time to come and see what we're about,' so we went over and introduced ourselves. Then we all went to the bar to get better acquainted and it was about this time that The Damned took to the stage. As I can remember they were going to play two sets, so the first one only lasted about 15 minutes, so we went back to the bar to find out more about Zeppelin. I was chatting away to Jimmy and Robert when a loud crashing sound was coming from the stage, so I went to see what was happening. I was amazed to find John stood at the back of the drum kit with an angry snarl on his face and, standing bolt upright, he let out a tirade of abuse at the band. He was shouting 'Where's the fucking band gone? They've only been playing for 15 minutes – we play for three fucking hours because we're real men and not a bunch of wimps. Where's that Mouse Scabies? I'll show him how to play, Bollocks, leave him where he is, I'll play with the band, and he carried on calling for the band to come back on.

Certain members of the Zeppelin entourage moved in to try and calm John down and get him off the stage. The funniest thing was that as they lifted John off the floor and started to carry him out to take him up the stairs, he was still bolt upright shouting for Mouse Scabies to come out. By this time the audience had returned to their original mood and were shouting 'Piss off you old hippie!'"

So exit John Bonham from the punk scene, and to think that at the ripe old age of 29, you're an old hippie. What was worse, in two years' time, as Zeppelin readied themselves for the Knebworth concerts, they would be called dinosaurs. How fickle the music industry can be.

As for Glenn Matlock, I recall with some amusement him telling me that, as a young lad learning to play guitar, he had saved all his pocket money so he could buy a music book to learn some chords to some top songs. One of the best guitarists, he reckoned, was Jimmy Page, so what better book to buy than Zeppelin's second album songbook. Racing home keen to get stuck in, he discovered with some astonishment that, "there weren't any fucking chords. It was all riffs."

The new wave stir caused the voices of doom to cry out that dinosaur bands like Led Zeppelin would no longer dominate and would disappear into the past from whence they'd come. Zep's 11th tour of America would prove this to be utter crap, never mind the bollocks. The tour was supposed to have started in February, but was postponed for over a month while Robert battled with a bout of tonsillitis.

With the responsibility of a young family, I had finally got myself a proper job as a salesman at Viscount Furniture, a large store in the rural town of Alcester, Warwickshire. So it came as a big surprise when, during the halt to Zeppelin's attack on the States, John and Pat arrived at the shop to give my career a little boost. Together they bought carpets, beds, suites and various other nic-nacs, adding up to more than the shop normally took in a week. The manager was so impressed he said I ought to lunch with them (my thoughts exactly) and off we went in John's latest purchase, a Mercedes 6-door limousine. John drove while Pat and I sat in the back watching TV and sipping champagne.

There was no way I was going back to work that day, so

after a good curry it was decided that we should pop over to see how Robert was getting on. Within a few minutes of arriving in Robert's lounge, several bottles of wine and a large bottle of brandy appeared. The rest of the day was spent with Robert and John reminiscing about times gone by and listening to a tape by Ral Donner, an artist Robert had got very excited about. By the end of the day, and the brandy, Robert decided he was going to scour the States for this fella and record him. John was also in a state of excitement, because at long last he'd been voted the Number One drummer in both the *NME* and *Sounds*. So here we were, the top drummer (world), top singer (world) and top furniture salesman (Alcester).

Finally on 1 April, Led Zeppelin kicked off that 11th tour of America at the Dallas Memorial Auditorium. Again it was their biggest tour, with 51 shows in some 30 cities, in front of a staggering 1.3million fans. They broke their attendance record when 76,229 people came to see them at the Pontiac Silverdome on 30 April. During the month of June they would play six nights at both The Forum in California and Madison Square Gardens, New York. The tour would run from April until August, with breaks at the beginning of May and July. Both times John flew home.

On John's second visit back home in July, two birthday parties were thrown at Old Hyde. One for me on the 13th, and another for Jason on the 15th. This time round it wouldn't just be Jason playing with a new toy as John had got one too, an AC Cobra. Still, as you'd expect, this was no ordinary Cobra, it was the bee's knees. COB1, originally owned and raced by Duncan Hamilton, a winner at Le Mans. It was a lovely sunny day, and John fancied putting it through its paces, so the pit crew lined up outside the Chequers pub and tanks were filled. A cloud of Mach One like smoke from the rear of the car announced the trials were over. The car had stopped on the side of the road and John never moved, so we raced up to see what was wrong. Arriving at the car we found John sat still, just staring at his latest pride and joy. "What's wrong?" we asked. "I've fucking broke it, that's what's wrong."

Luckily it was nothing major, so John flew back to America, still a happy man, not knowing that trouble and heartache were just around the corner. On the first night of two at the Oakland Stadium, John was involved in a fight with security guards, along with Peter Grant, John Bindon and Richard Cole, following an incident with Peter's young son Warren. All four were arrested and charged with battery, but all this would be overshadowed by the news that Karac, Robert's young son, had died in hospital. Robert, accompanied by John, flew home immediately.

Chapter 22

J.H. BONHAM DEVELOPMENTS (INCORPORATING BODGIT AND SCARPER)

Arriving back at the farm, John immersed himself in family life, getting more and more involved in Jason's scrambling. There was still a gap and he needed to do something during the week, so he called in to see me at the shop.

"Mick, I've got this idea. How about getting all the lads who worked on Old Hyde and getting back into the building business?"

"What we gonna do?" I asked.

"Renovate old farms."

"Whose?"

"Mine. I just bought one."

"What's the wages?"

"30 bob a week and a big orange at Christmas."

"Done."

It was down to Jacko and me to round up the old team. Stan Blick and his son Pete were the brickies, Tuffy Reeves and his son Andy handled groundwork and roofing, whilst Jacko and I were basically carpenter and chief cook and bottle washer. And as of 5 September, J.H. Bonham Developments was back in business and our first project was a derelict old house known as Beech Elm Farm, adjacent to Old Hyde.

Once the team were all assembled we arrived at Beech Elm Farm to view the new project. What we saw left us wondering whether John really knew what he was doing. The word derelict doesn't come near to what state the house was in. Derelict would have been easy, this place had fallen down. The front wall was now in the garden and the main bedroom was now on the ground floor next to the lounge. Closer inspection revealed that the barns and outbuildings were in better condition, so that's where we started, firstly securing a shanty for us and a nice office for the gaffer.

Over the next three years we would renovate three farms altogether, incorporating a lot of hard work and several excursions into silliness. Yet again, one of these episodes would involve John's right hand man Mathew. Along with his many other chores, Matt had to tend to the chickens that were now living at Old Hyde, producing fresh eggs. Unknown to Matt, on the other farm Tuffy had found a dead fox that was as stiff as a board and, along with John, had devised a devilishly good plan. Before I carry on with the story, I'll try and introduce you to 'Tuffy'. Always adorned in a flat cap, he was a man of the land, a wheeler-dealer countryman, small in stature but huge in character with a very dry sense of humour. John and I had known him since we were kids, because he had worked for our Granddad and then for Jacko, but in all this time we had never knew his first name, he was always just 'Tuffy'.

Anyway, back to the devilish plan: the fox was taken up to John's house, and with the use of a stick he was propped upright in the chicken coop. The chickens were put out of harm's way and we all took cover behind a wall. Once under cover, John shouted out for Matt, telling him to get the gun, as there was a fox after the chickens. Within seconds Mathew was out of the house, gun at the ready and running towards the hen house. KABOOM! A shot was fired into the air to scare the fox, but it hadn't worked as the fox stood his ground, much to Matt's disbelief. As he slowly approached the fox, the stick gradually broke and poor old foxy slowly fell over and ended up with his legs sticking up in the air. All was deathly quiet, broken by inane giggling from behind the wall. Still, no harm done, except that the noise of the gun had scared the shit out of Bruno the bull, while he was going about the business those bulls do best. It took nigh on a week before that cow stopped smiling.

As Beech Elm rose out of the rubble, John was so chuffed he went and acquired another derelict farm for our next project. He spent his days sorting out the plans for the new job and coming up with new ideas for Beech Elm, then on most weekends he would go off with Pat to watch Jason scramble as part of a team he now sponsored. With all his involvement in the building business and Jason's scrambling, John seemed more relaxed than he'd been for some time. Yet there were still a couple of issues that worried him. What would become of the band? And if they didn't play for some time, would they be forgotten? Answers to these questions came early in 1978 when Led Zeppelin made a virtual clean sweep of the awards in the *Cream* magazine Reader's Poll in America.

On 14 March, John had to go to London for three days of meetings with the rest of Led Zeppelin. To my delight he asked if I would like to accompany him as well. Well, do bears shit in the woods? Now I thought the trip down in the Porsche was good enough, but when we arrived at the Swan Song offices in London, a chauffeur driven Rolls Royce limo had been laid on to take us wherever we wanted to go. We were running late so it was straight out of one car and into the other and off we went to the first meeting, in a large, tastefully designed office overlooking the Thames. Around a highly polished wooden table sat lawyers, accountants and all the members of Led Zeppelin, discussing financial packages. I thought they were talking telephone numbers so just sat there looking stupid and thinking that there should have been a sign over the door saying 'Be Bop spoken here'. Once the meeting was over it was back to Swan Song for beers and a bite to eat.

"I'm going tae the chippy, d'yee want anything?" – it was not so much a question, more an order in a raucous Scottish accent. I could only stammer "Yes please." This was my first introduction to Maggie Bell, a great lady who would become a great friend. That evening, while all the members of the band converged on Richard Cole's flat, I stayed with Maggie and the two girls who worked in the office, Unity and Cynthia. We met up with all the others at a nightclub called J. Arthurs, where we drank and danced until the early hours. John had left a couple of hours earlier, so it was Maggie who managed to get me back to the Kensington Garden Hotel at about 4.00am. By about 5.00am I had finally managed to find my room and was rewarded for my efforts with a bottle of champagne on ice.

John would be at meetings all the following day and I would be surplus to requirements, which allowed me to make a gradual return to the life of the living. Some fresh air was needed so I took a steady walk to the office in the hope of a quiet afternoon. Upon my arrival Unity introduced me to John Bindon, whose job it was to make sure nothing untoward happened to John or any other member of the band; the Minder. As he told me about his job with John and some of the incidents he'd been involved with, I felt a definite feeling that he was a man that could do his job and do it well. So it came as no surprise that when he rang the local pub and ordered beers for us, the barman delivered them to us in the office. Late in the afternoon I was collected by John's personal assistant Rex King and taken to meet John at the Water Rat pub further down Kings Road. The evening was spent chatting and I got talking to a guy who went by the name of Tom The Fib, who told me all about his escapades with the Emperor of Mexico's son. He was bloody good too. Shit, he had me believing him.

When the pub closed John was going to a club with a few others, but not wanting another night like the previous one, I declined the invite and went back to the office for a nightcap. Still, just like the previous night I was deposited at the hotel just as most people were starting to make their way to work. Our last day in town was spent travelling from one meeting to another, until at 8.00pm we eventually set off for home, taking Robert and Maureen with us.

One thing that had been decided during the London trip was that the band would get together to rehearse for a new album and, on 2 May, the band members convened at Clearwell Castle, set in the Forest Of Dean near the Welsh border for a musical get-together. On 3 October, John would once again meet up with John Paul Jones, this time at Abbey Road studios, to record two tracks with Paul McCartney and Wings. The two tracks were 'Glad to See You Here' and 'The Rockestra Theme' for the forthcoming album 'Back to the Egg'. Other artists at the session included Pete Townsend, Hank Marvin and Dave Gilmour. As soon as the session finished, it was back to rehearsals with Led Zeppelin before they would fly off to Stockholm to record their ninth album at ABBA's Polar Studios.

During a break in rehearsals, John had gone to see Reg and Chrissie Jones' new band Grit, which also featured Ace Kefford on bass, play at Shenstone College. Also in the audience was John's old mate Johnny Hill and it wasn't long before the two John's were onstage backing the Jones' boys. Way of Life played once more.

Chapter 23

SCRAMBLE ON

With all the breaks in John's music career, he would spend a great deal of his time working with Jason and the Kawasaki Schoolboy Team at many of the meetings, arranged by the West Mercia Schoolboy Scrambling Club. He also helped sponsor some of the meetings, to help raise money for many different causes. His biggest was at Hawkstone Park, a hard and testing championship course near Whitchurch, Shropshire. As with all the other projects like the band and the farm, it was my job to record the events on film. During the races a major problem had happened to Jason's bike and the part that was needed was at Alec Wright's house in London. Mathew and I would have to take it in turns driving to London and back, a 350-mile round trip, with strict instructions from John not to stop for any reason. We kept the accelerator to the floor all the way there, which put us well ahead of schedule, so I managed to talk Mathew into stopping for a bite to eat, on the understanding that no one told John. Arriving back at the track John remarked on what great time we'd made. I was so chuffed I piped up, "Yeah, and we even stopped for some grub."

Whack!!

This surprised me because John hadn't moved. It had been Mathew who was stood behind me. It was a fair whack too, right across the head. If that wasn't bad enough we were told that ten minutes after we'd set off for London they'd discovered the part was not needed. As for stopping, the following day Mathew and I were given the job of emptying the toilets. Lovely. Now let me get my hands on the prat who said, 'Where there's muck there's money.' Still, the meeting was a success and we'd be back in a couple of months.

On November 3rd we returned to Hawkstone Park and this time John would come up with one of his best ideas to date. To get some really good photos he decided that I should lie under the Girling Leap and film the bikes flying through the air above me. To all you non Motor X types, the Girling Leap is a jump with a drop of about five feet, and all these young lads come tear-arsing round the corner then gun over the jump, careering through the air for God knows how far. Well, John thought it was a good idea, so I did it, lying on my back with camera pointing skywards waiting for John to give the signal that a bike was approaching. By the time that signal came I didn't know whether it was my heart or my arse that was giving me palpitations, but by the time I'd opened my eyes and clicked the shutter twice the bike had gone. Still, it didn't stop two members of St. John Ambulance rushing over because they thought a bike had knocked down some poor old bastard.

The day ended with everyone going to a nearby hotel for a meal and a shufty at the disco upstairs. During the evening's entertainment it was announced that there would be a drinking race. With words of encouragement from John along the lines of, "Go on our kid you'll piss it" off I went. Strong in arm, thick in head, onto the stage with four other unsuspecting idiots. What they hadn't told us was that what we actually had to drink was half a pint of cold baked beans, but the prize was a large bottle of champagne. Anyway, I did it, I won it and we drank the champers. I fell over and didn't come round until about 2.00am. As my aching eyes scanned a room I had never seen before I began to panic. What I didn't know was that John had booked me a room at the hotel and then, like everyone else, had gone home. Panic turned to fear as I remembered that Lin was expecting me home yesterday and I couldn't even get out of the hotel because it was all locked up. After making enough noise to wake the dead, an irate proprietor appeared in his pyjamas and kicked my arse out the door. Thank you. As well as helping to sponsor the team, John was also involved with launching the Superkids' charity, which would raise money for disabled children during scramble meetings and other functions. At one of these events he would raffle his chopper bike he'd used in 'The Song Remains the Same' to raise even more cash. And yet with all this going on, John never lost his enthusiasm for playing drums, with anybody and anywhere. During that year he'd played with Zep at Clearwell Castle, Paul McCartney at the Abbey Road studios and even Way of Life at Shenstone College. And on 24 November he got up and played with a local band, for the second time, at the Annual Presentation Dinner for the Scramble Club.

"The band had appeared at Stourport Civic Hall for a Scramble Presentation Night with Dave Thorpe, a top scrambler at the time, presenting the awards," recalls Dennis Williams, the manager of the band in question. "During the evening it was made known to me that John Bonham and his family were in the building. When the lads were told they all crapped themselves with nerves, but then excelled themselves, knowing that such a superstar was in the audience."

"I approached John during the break and asked if he would like a session with the lads, who were known as the GB Band (John Allen, Steve Wills, Malcolm Evans and Steve Lees). I must confess that after hearing and reading all the bad press about him I thought he would tell me to get lost. The response was the complete opposite. His face lit up and he eagerly accepted the invitation. Turning to the drummer he told him to tighten the clamps on his kit as tight as he could. At this Steve Lees looked worried, thinking his recently paid for kit was going to be wrecked. John assured him that if he damaged anything he would get him a new kit. Soon there was a buzz around the place and then a roar of approval when John took to the stage. He played a couple of numbers with Steve Lees desperately trying to keep his kit clamped together and then he brought Jason on stage for a knock. Watching him play at such a young age you sensed that he would be in the same mould as his father. He excelled and the crowd responded with a standing ovation for both the Bonhams.

"Looking back on that night, could John be that bad guy the press loved to smear, or a very talented family man who took great pleasure in giving his friends a treat and liked to show off the talents of his son Jason? I know that John Bonham was the latter man. After the gig his friends outnumbered the hangers on, but he still took time to chat with the lads, encouraging them and answering all their cheeky questions.

"That night was a great experience for the lads, who were still in their early twenties, and who would have thought it would happen again a mere 12 months later. When I heard there would be another presentation the following year I pulled out all the stops to get the gig on the off-chance John might be in attendance once again. As the date drew nearer, the feedback about a possible appearance from John was good so this time we went with cameras. The venue was Mount Olympus, Stourport, and sure enough, John was there and this time he approached us asking if he could repeat last year's session. Who could refuse? It was a repeat in every way, with the crowd going wild, Jason taking the stage and drummer Steve still panicking about his drums. It was a dream come true not once but twice. Sadly it didn't happen a third time, but John was a local lad who'd made the big time but never forgot his family or his mates."

LULU INTERVIEW 1999

Q: How did you rate John as a drummer?

L: John was the most awesome drummer, a genius; I don't think I've seen a drummer to compare with John.

Q: Did you meet up very often?

L: When in London recording, he would visit our house along with Robert Plant, Keith Moon and Ringo Starr. Brother Billy and Maurice would be there and we would party into the night. I would hang out as long as possible, trying to be one of the boys. It was great fun whenever we met.

Q: I understand you had some great holidays with Pat and John, was he a fun person to be with?

L: People said things about John, which I could not believe; I never saw it in all the time I knew him. We went on holiday to the South of France with Pat and John and had a fantastic holiday. When we stayed with them they were the perfect hosts even giving up their bedroom so we would be more comfortable. While we were there we met their son Jason who at six was an incredible talent playing drums like a guy many years older.

Q: How would you like people to remember John?

L: John and I had a lot in common, it was not about being a star, or about doing it to become rich and famous, it was doing it because it's in every fibre of your body, and that's why I think it's kind of sweet that I am able to say I knew him. John was very generous, and incredibly passionate, which allowed him to play the way he did.

Chapter 24

A QUIET GAME OF CHEQUERS

1979 began at a nice relaxed pace; working on farms, going to scrambles and drinking at the Chequers pub. Located a mile down the road from Old Hyde in the village of Cutnall Green, The Chequers was another of those olde worlde pubs we favoured, with stoned floors and a landlord to match. Kenny Powell, a notorious character, became good friends with John, owing to the fact that, when it came to looning around, he was up there with the best of them. So if anything untoward was going on, Kenny was probably involved, as we were to find out on more than one occasion.

On 4 January, John had received tickets for the State Express Snooker Tournament, being held at the Albany Hotel in Birmingham, and thought it would be a nice treat for Jacko, who was a big snooker fan. Kenny joined us for this sporting night out and, on completion of the match, we were all invited into the player's lounge for a drink and a chat. John hit it off with Alex Higgins from the outset and they both became very merry, drinking Planters Punch, whilst Jacko was introduced to six times World Champion Ray Reardon and was happily having his photo taken with him. Towards the end of the session we all posed for a picture with Arthur Askey, a legend of British comedy and Leslie Crowther, the TV personality who sadly passed away several years ago.

The evening had been a great success until a very stern looking official entered the room and demanded to know "Who does he belong to?" pointing back into the snooker room. We ventured into the auditorium only to find he was referring to Kenny, who had drunk up, curled up and gone to sleep on the tournament match table.

Later that same month, after working on a very cold morning at Wood Farm, John and I decided to call in at Chequers to get warm and grab a bit to eat. Discussing the weather with Ken, I told them my solution to keeping warm; wearing long-John style underwear, I realised that I should have kept that to myself after becoming the butt end of all John and Ken's jokes, as well as any other punter within earshot. So much interest had been shown in my underwear that Ken said he would bet me ten quid that I didn't have the bottle to dance around the pub in the said underwear, a bet that doubled when John put a tenner in too. Working on the theory that nothing from nothing leaves twenty quid, the kecks were off, the music was on and I was dancing around the tables. All was fine until pay-up time; John gave me his but Kenny had disappeared. Then John disappeared but soon returned carrying a large sledgehammer. After a couple of gentle taps on the bar John shouted, "Bring the money Ken or the bar gets it." The money appeared, but not Ken. It transpired that while these shenanigans were going on, the landlord had spotted his wife returning from shopping, and being a born again coward had disappeared upstairs and gotten into bed. When questioned by his wife he claimed not to know anything about what was happening downstairs. Just another lunchtime at the Chequers.

During the time John would be hitching up the trailer and taking Jason to the scrambles, Jacko would be doing the same, but his trailer was a horsebox and his passengers were our sister Debbie and her trusty old steed Mustang. On the weekends that she spent with Jacko they would tour the gymkhanas and horse shows. With Debbie's knowledge of horses, and after the Old Sam debacle, John had asked her to come with us to have a look at a horse he wanted to buy. The horsebox was hitched up and we all set off to Whitchurch to check out this horse. After an inspection, Debbie advised John that it was a perfect beast so we brought it back home. During the drive back John suddenly turned on the radio as the intro to a song called 'Roxanne' by The Police came on. During the breaks in our vocal accompaniment John raved about the band and the great technique of the drummer, saying he reckoned they would be the band to knock Zep off the top spot. As we carried on our singsong, Debbie was still unaware that the horse behind us was hers, but as John told her the news, she looked up tearfully and said, "I'm going to call him Achillies." It was a great day that ended in total joy for our sister.

Although John loved this period of his life, he was a drummer through to the bone, so when he heard that Zep was booked to do a major gig at Knebworth, his face beamed. As the date of 4 August drew near though, doubts began to creep into his mind. After two years away from playing live, could Led Zeppelin still pull the big crowd?

Previous page and above
The lucky ones, Knebworth 1979, the
last UK concert for Led Zeppelin

Chapter 25

THE SUN SHINES AGAIN

On 28 May John left the country life and returned to work, rehearsing with Led Zeppelin. The new album, 'In Through the Out Door' would be released to coincide with the Knebworth shows and the fact that the American public had just voted them top band in no less than eight categories in *Circus* magazine, helped to allay John's fears.

For me, the biggest gig of 1979 was at Bromsgrove Hospital, where on 1 July Lin would squeeze the shit out of my hand for a second time as she gave life to our son, James Colin Bonham. The name had been chosen so there would be another JB and his middle name, after his godfather Colin Andrews. We hadn't considered that his initials would be JCB, also a large mechanical excavator, so he began life being known as 'little digger' by the nurses.

After a couple of weeks' break looking after my family, I returned to work, just in time to take John and Robert to Birmingham Airport. Nervously they boarded a private jet and took off for their first performance in two years, at the Falkoner Theater in Copenhagen. It had been ten years since they'd last played there.

Ticket demand for the Knebworth Festival had been so great that the 150,000 tickets had sold out, so a second performance would be scheduled for the following week.

On my way to John's house on the morning of Saturday 4 August, I called in at a newsagent to pick up the music papers, to see if there was anything about Zep, just as I had done virtually every week since 1968. There was a great piece titled 'The Sun Shines Again' in *Record Mirror* by Robin Smith and when I showed it to John it made his day. At lunchtime Mathew and I jumped into my 'Chevy (not a real one mind you, a Vauxhall

Chevette) and headed down to Knebworth. John, Pat and Jason were to follow us down but when John went past us at warp speed we decided we'd catch up with him later. By the time we found the hotel in Stevenage, John said we might as well go directly to the site. As we drove down the dirt road to the stage area we were staggered by the size of the crowd. The Zeppelin Army had arrived in force and was gathered in front of the stage waiting for the main event. Flags and banners from all over were held aloft – it was a fantastic scenario.

Once we were settled in the large caravan provided for the band we made plans for the afternoon. John had told Debbie that she couldn't come to the concert because she was too young, but they would do plenty of indoor shows later that year and she could come to those. Not one to be fobbed off, she decided she was not about to miss this one, so with iron-will determination, and much to the alarm of our Mum, Debbie bought a ticket and travelled down with friends Neville Farmer and Eddie Murphy (no not that one) and was somewhere out in the crowd. She told me years later that she would never have gone against his wishes but for the fact she had some strange feeling that if she didn't see him then, she never would again.

After seeing the number of people out there, and knowing his kid sister was out there, John got worried. He suggested that we ought to go up on stage and look for her. Even with the binoculars I had with me I knew it was going to be tricky, it was like looking for a needle in a haystack. John and I took turns with the glasses until he had to go to get ready, but he told me to keep looking.

While we were on stage John found me what he thought looked like a great place to position myself with the camera when the band took to the stage, and having given up the search for Debbie we made our way back to the caravan to spend what time was left to sit in the sun and catch up with everyone as they arrived. The crowd was being warmed up by bands like Fairport Convention, featuring John's old Way of Life mate Dave Pegg, closely

followed by Chas and Dave. I also managed to get back on stage in time to see Southside Johnny and the Asbury Dukes play a superb set.

At around 8.00pm I took my position and got the camera ready. After a lengthy wait Led Zeppelin appeared on stage to a tumultuous roar. All four band members looked slightly hesitant as they took their positions. As I focused my camera on John's kit I couldn't help thinking why there were loads of people around the stage but no one near me. The answer came as the boys launched into 'The Song Remains the Same'; John had stuck me in front of a very powerful lighting rig and within minutes my jacket was steaming. I was the only photographer sat in their own microwave, and what made things worse was that there was nowhere else to go, so it was grin and bear it time. With a PA system of 60,000 watts and a lighting rig of 100,000 watts, most of it shining through me, the show was pretty spectacular. Looking back I can now understand why John kept giving me funny looks. I must have looked like an X-ray. Some three hours later after several encores, and being cooked on both sides, I left the stage drenched, along with four very happy musicians.

While everyone sat around cooling off it was reported that there was a commotion outside with a young girl. Apparently one of the security guards had thrown her against the fence after she had repeatedly pestered him to let her into the compound, claiming she was Bonzo's sister. Richard Cole immediately went to fetch her, giving the security guard a right bollocking. John also made his way to her. As she walked in, she saw John and ran to him. He in turn picked her up in the air and hugged her. He then bollocked her for coming down on her own and causing us all so much worry. Still, we were all more than pleased to see her.

After the show, Led Zeppelin and co had been invited to a celebration party at the big house at Knebworth. In a long elegant dining room a banqueting table had been laid out fit for visiting royalty. In a rather splendid party atmosphere we ate and drank with the heirachy until, and

Opposite
Robert Plant at Knebworth

I don't know who did it but, the first bun was thrown. A marvellous end to a marvellous day.

As we travelled back to the hotel, along the A1, we beheld a sight that would soften even the hardest man. All along the road, for as far as the eye could see, were the Zep army returning home, victorious but knackered. Small fires lit the faces of thousands of countless fans as they prepared for the hitch home. Some had fallen asleep where they lay, some were in sleeping bags, others in tents. At seeing this remarkable sight, John proclaimed, "These are the people we owe it all to, and if I could I'd take them all back to the hotel," after which he wound down the car window, stuck out his hands and applauded 'The Ocean'.

Back at the hotel, being pretty out of it, I fell into bed and sank into a deep sleep, only to be woken at some ungodly hour by a heavy thumping on my door. On opening it, I discovered it was one of G's minders looking like someone built from a blacksmith's anvil. He instructed me that Mr Grant wanted to see me. Oh shit. Memories of school flooded back about being summoned to the headmasters' study and thinking, "Oh no, not the cane".

"Matt, Matt, wake up, G wants to see me!" I said in a tone somewhere between fear and terror. "Ooooh fuck," he replied and went straight back to sleep. As I made my way to Peter's room I noticed that it was 4.30am, so I figured this must be pretty serious.

"Ah, young Bonzo!" declared the band's manager. "Is John going straight to the scramble with Pat and Jason in the morning?"

"You mean you got me out of bed at 4.30 in the morning just to ask me that!" Of course, I only said this to myself then politely answered, "Yes, I think so," and scurried back to my room. By the time I arose from my pit the next day, everyone had indeed departed, and I drove home happy in the knowledge this would all happen again next week, and it would be Jacko's turn to accompany John. I just hoped he'd enjoy the band from a cooler vantage point than I would.

Above
John's last UK performance with
Led Zeppelin, August 1979

Above
Pete Townsend and Paul McCartney
at the Concert for Kampuchea

Above
John Paul Jones

Many music critics would slag off the Knebworth gigs but they were outnumbered by the fans that had voted with their feet. When a crowd of 150,000 are screaming for more, who are you going to listen to? It would be these fans that put 'In Through the Out Door' at the top of the album charts around the world, with a record seven weeks at Number One in America. Coupled with the fact that Led Zeppelin again scored seven Number Ones in the *Melody Maker* poll, the comeback had succeeded with a scoreline of: Fans 1, Critics Nil.

No matter what the critics said, I had thoroughly enjoyed it and it would remain clear in my mind for the rest of my life because, although not knowing it at the time, it would be the last time I would see John playing with Led Zeppelin.

The rest of the year saw John spending a lot of time in London at meetings with the band, discussing future plans including a possible tour next year, and along with Robert and John Paul Jones, collecting their *Melody Maker* Awards. John's love of fast cars was rekindled whilst on a trip to Adrian Hamiltons to get the Range Rover serviced and bring back the Roller. There was a beautiful Ferrari Dino in the showroom, so we brought that back as well.

During October, nerves were beginning to show as another christening loomed on the horizon. This time there were strict instructions of "go out this time you can lock the door behind you". James' christening was held in the best possible taste. The service was held at the same church as before, but this time, at the party afterwards, the food stayed on the plates and we stayed in the house.

On 12 December we called in at the Birmingham Odeon to see Wings. After the show we met up with them backstage, where I felt well and truly out of my depth. I had grown up with the Beatles and was a great admirer of Paul's work. After John introduced me to the members of Wings I shrank back into the corner. Feeling a bit like a dustman at a Royal Garden Party, Linda

Above
Billy Connolly

Above
Paul McCartney

McCartney came over and asked if I was all right and then went and fetched me a drink and some food. Whether Linda had sensed how I was feeling or not, she made me feel so relaxed and we spent a long time talking about photography, the band and life in general. I came away from that gig totally blown away, because you couldn't help loving Linda McCartney, a lovely lady I would always remember. Two weeks later we would meet up again at the Rock for Kampuchea concert in London, and again Linda came over to make sure I was okay. Treasured memories.

John was already in London at rehearsals with the Rockestra, so I picked up Pat and Mathew and drove down to Blakes Hotel to meet up with him before the show. The gig was at the Hammersmith Odeon and would feature Elvis Costello, The Clash, Rockpile, Wings and culminate with The Rockestra. As usual it was my job to take some photos of the event, which gave me an ideal vantage point to watch the show. The MC for the night was Billy Connolly who, while waiting for all the members of The Rockestra to congregate on stage, decides to do an impromptu strip. Luckily for us all, the call went out that the band was ready before Billy had gone the whole hog.

The curtain went up to reveal a myriad of superstars. There were all of Wings, Pete Townsend and Kenney Jones from The Who, Dave Edmunds of Rockpile, James Honeyman Scott from The Pretenders and Plant, Jones and Bonham from Led Zeppelin. My problem as photographer was that John was so high up at the back of the stage I could just make out his top hat bobbing up and down. Still, it didn't detract from the great playing as the band ripped through 'the Rockestra Theme', followed by The Beatles' 'Let It Be' and climaxed with Little Richard's 'Lucille'. After the show we returned to Blakes, along with Jonesy, who was also staying there, and upon finding a small bar with a piano, we finished off the evening singing some old classics with great backing by John Paul Jones.

Chapter 26

A NEW DECADE AND THE END OF AN ERA

With the success of Knebworth and the 'In Through the Out Door' album it was inevitable that Led Zeppelin would go back out and tour. So it came as no surprise when John returned from a meeting in London and excitedly announced the band would be touring throughout Europe during the summer.

Rehearsals started in April at The Rainbow in Finsbury Park, London, and as an added boost, Cream magazine announced Zep had topped no less than 15 categories in their reader's poll. All was well with the band. After rehearsing for a week they switched venues to The New Victoria Theatre, to keep the press in the dark about their plans. During a break in rehearsals Robert came to see me at the farm and said that I was to do some photos of the band rehearsing and then go on tour with them. It seemed like a dream come true for me, but alas, it was the last I ever heard about the idea, so on 17 June Led Zeppelin embarked on their first European tour since the early 70s, but I did not. This tour would see a re-invigorated Zeppelin play a string of 14 dates in Germany, Belgium and Switzerland, but once more misfortune struck, when after three dates at Nuremberg, John collapsed during the show, which had to be cancelled. Though not 100 per cent fit, John completed the tour, which would see the last ever Led Zeppelin gig at the Eisspothalle in Berlin on 7 July, 1980.

Arriving back home on the 9th, John seemed in good spirits, and gave Jacko some good news that would make him a very happy man. On 31 July he was to make his home at the cottage at Old Hyde. Nothing else John could have done would have meant more to his father. In need of a family holiday, I took John, Pat, Jason and Zoe to Birmingham Airport to catch a private plane down to the South of France for a month's holiday throughout

August. I then returned home and took my family for a holiday to the Isle of Wight.

Everything seemed well with the world. John was on holiday with his family. I was on holiday with my family. And Jacko was happily decorating his new home, with paint that *we* had supplied this time.

On 9 September we all met up again at Wood Farm, refreshed and ready to go. The holiday, it seemed, had been just what the doctor ordered for John, who was in buoyant mood and looking forward to the next tour of the States. After getting things underway at Wood Farm, John and I went up to the cottage to help Jacko finish decorating his home.

On a beautiful sunny morning, John arrived on site early and in a very cheerful mood and thought it would be a good idea to get all the cars washed and polished. It was Wednesday, 24 September and he was eager to get them out of the way before setting off for Jimmy's house in Windsor to start rehearsals. At lunchtime John's personal assistant Rex King arrived at the farm to take him down to London. As they disappeared down the long driveway I waved 'Our Kid' goodbye.

Chapter 27

WHAT IS AND WHAT SHOULD NEVER BE

"Love is like, my old piano." Diana Ross was singing her latest hit on *Top of the Pops* when the telephone rang. On lifting the receiver, the only words I heard were, "Come over to the farm straight away." My father was speaking them and he could barely get the words out for crying.

I'll never forget that moment. It became frozen in time, like a scene from a film and is as clear today as it was back then. In all my years I had never heard or seen Dad cry and I knew it meant that something had happened to a very close member of the family.

The journey to Old Hyde normally took 20 minutes, but tonight seemed like an eternity as the question, "What's happened?" continually raced through my mind. It didn't take long to work out when I arrived, because security guards stood at either side of the gate and Robert Plant was waiting for me. He told me to leave my car and walk up the drive with him. As he did so, he gently broke the news to me that John had died some time during the previous night. I don't know how to explain the impact his words had on me in that split second and how I felt afterwards. But as I sat with my family the only thing I knew was that the brother I loved so much, my life long hero, was gone.

My only respite from the nightmare came, as ever, from Lin, who held me tight for the rest of the night while I tried to make sense of it all.

After a family service at Rushock Church, the funeral procession made its way to Worcester Crematorium for the final service. That afternoon I said goodbye to Our Kid for the last time, and then returned to Chequers, along with family, friends and showbiz colleagues to toast his short but incredible life. As I sat there, allowing the events of the past few weeks to sink in, it wasn't the best time for Benji Le Fevre to start winding me up. I put him on his arse and legged it out the door. After calming down, I re-entered the pub through a back door, and joined Mathew sitting at the bar. He just looked at me through tearful eyes and said, "John would be proud of you. He would have enjoyed that."

What more is there to say? Only that we try to deal with the devastation of his death on a day-to-day basis. When Jacko died at the Farm in 1989, I realised during the service, held in the same church, that he had never gotten over it. As I looked at Mum, I knew she never would. I know I never will. I miss him and Dad so much.

It seemed like a lifetime had gone full circle as I sat and chatted with John Hill during the writing of this book, the chap who had started it all those years ago.

CHRONOLOGY

1966

Jimmy Page joins The Yardbirds, initially as bass player.

John Bonham joins Way of Life, his first band.

John Bonham (aged 17) marries Pat Phillips.

Robert Plant joins Listen, formerly known as The Tennessee Teens.

1967

John Bonham plays with Robert Plant in The Crawling King Snakes.

Bonham takes over from John Trickett in The Band of Joy, with Robert Plant and Kevyn Gammond.

The Band of Joy record demo discs at Regent Sound Studios in London.

1968

8 February. The first London appearance of Band of Joy featuring Bonham and Plant at the Marquee Club in London, supporting Edwin Starr.

Band of Joy split up in the spring of 1968.

In 1968 Robert Plant records a track called 'Operator' with Alexis Korner and Steve Miller (on piano).

John Bonham tours in the UK with Tim Rose.

August. First rehearsals of Led Zeppelin.

October. 'Led Zeppelin 1' recorded at Olympic Studios in 30 hours.

15 October. The debut UK concert of Led Zeppelin at Surrey University.

October–December. Led Zeppelin on tour.

November. Led Zeppelin play at a Middle Earth presentation concert at the Roundhouse in London, with John Lee Hooker and The Deviants billed as 'The Yardbirds now known as Led Zeppelin'.

10 December. Led Zeppelin play at London's Marquee Club for a fee of £150.

20 December. Led Zeppelin perform at the Wood Green Fishmongers Hall, London.

26 December. Debut concert in USA supporting the MC5 and Vanilla Fudge at The Boston Tea Party.

1969

In 1969 John Bonham buys a house in West Hagley, and Robert Plant buys Jennings Farm at Blakeshall, Wolverley near Kidderminster.

January. Concerts in USA including three nights at the Fillmore West with Country Joe and the Fish.

17 January. 'Led Zeppelin 1' released in USA. The album enters the charts at number 98.

January–August. Recording for the second LP at several studios.

31 January and 1 February. Led Zeppelin appear at the Fillmore East with Iron Butterfly headlining.

February. Short tour of Scandinavia.

March. Club tour of the UK billed as The New Yardbirds at some venues.
Also played at the Wood Tavern in Hornsey, with admission priced at seven shillings and sixpence.

21 March. Only UK television appearance on BBC programme *How Late It Is*

March. A film and sound recording was made at a warehouse in Staines , Middlesex, featuring Eric Clapton, Jack Bruce, Stephen Stills, Roland Kirk, Buddy Guy, Colosseum, MJQ and Buddy Miles. This is now available on DVD but does not include footage of Led Zeppelin who were at the event.

1 April. 'Led Zeppelin 1' released in the UK.

1969 cont'd
April. Return to the USA for a tour including two nights at the Fillmore East in New York, supported by Woody Herman and his Orchestra.

June. Start of the first UK tour.

28 June. An afternoon performance at the Bath Festival of Blues held at the Bath Recreation Ground, sharing the bill with John Mayall, Fleetwood Mac, The Nice and John Hiseman's Colosseum, Taste and Chicken Shack.

July. Begin work on 'Led Zeppelin 2' at studios in Willesden.
Tour of the USA through until August.

22 October. 'Led Zeppelin 2' released.

November. Start of a tour of the USA with support acts including Isaac Hayes and Roland Kirk.

December. Awarded platinum and gold discs for sales of 'Led Zeppelin 1' and 'Led Zeppelin 2'.
Release of 'Whole Lotta Love' as a UK single cancelled by Peter Grant.

John Bonham: "There was a bit of a mix-up. We never wanted to put it out in England. It was only for American AM radio stations to promote the LP and that was a full-length version. In England they pressed up an edited version, and we want to release a single that we feel won't be a con."

In 1969 all of the members of Led Zeppelin played on the PJ Proby LP 'Three Week Hero' on 'You Shook Me' and John Paul Jones produced some of the tracks.

1970

January–August. Recording for the third LP at Olympic Sound in London and a studio in Memphis.

January. 'Led Zeppelin 2' knocks The Beatles' 'Abbey Road' LP off the number one chart slot in America, and reaches number one in England.

A UK tour starts at Birmingham Town Hall, with a concert at The Royal Albert Hall later in the month.

21 February. Led Zeppelin appear as 'Nobs' in Copenhagen, following a complaint from Count Evan von Zeppelin about the use of the family name.

March. Start of the sixth tour of America.

April. A rare TV appearance: Jimmy Page plays 'White Summer' and 'Black Mountain Side' on the *Julie Felix Show* on BBC 2.

April and May. Page and Plant go to a cottage in Snowdonia, Wales called Bron-Y-Aur, to begin writing what would become 'Led Zeppelin 3'.

John Bonham: "We're slackening off the pressure so we can work more in England."

June. Concerts in Iceland.

28 June. Perform to 200,000 people at the Bath Festival

of Blues and Progressive Music. Led Zeppelin went on stage at sunset.

This was held at the Bath and West Showground, Shepton Mallet over two days, and included Fairport Convention, Colosseum, Johnny Winter, Pink Floyd, Santana, Dr John, Mothers of Invention, Jefferson Airplane and Steppenwolf.

1970 cont'd

In 1969 Jimmy Page and John Bonham played on six tracks for the the LP 'Lord Sutch and Heavy Friends': Wailing Sounds, Cause I Love You, Flashing Lights, Thumping Beat, Union Jack Car and Baby Come Back. The album also featured Jeff Beck and Noel Redding and was released in 1970.

July. Tour of Germany.

August. Some concerts in America, and mixing of 'Led Zeppelin 3'.

5 October. Release of 'Led Zeppelin 3'.

December. First recording sessions for 'Led Zeppelin 4'. Work continued until August 1971 at Island Studios in London, Headley Grange and Los Angeles.

1971

January. Recording continues at Headley Grange in Hampshire.

March. UK tour begins and songs which will appear on 'Led Zeppelin 4' are premiered.

April. Live broadcast on John Peel's Radio One Sunday show.

May. Tour of France. There was a riot at a show in Milan when fans fought with riot police.

October. Tour of Japan, including a charity concert for victims of the atombomb attack of 1945.

November. UK tour including two nights at the Empire Pool Wembley on 20th and 21st with Bronco (featuring Kevyn Gammond), Stone the Crows and some circus acts.

8 November. Led Zeppelin 4/ Four Symbols released.

In 1971 there were also concerts at The Ulster Hall Belfast and The Boxing Stadium in Dublin. In Dublin, Phil Carson, the head of Atlantic Records in London, sat in with the band on bass guitar.

John Bonham: "We had a lot of time at home to think, and we grew a lot closer together. We kept seeing stories about us breaking up, but in reality we had never been closer together. We did so much in such a short space of time we got drained. We needed a break before we got stale."

1972

In 1972 John Bonham bought The Old Hyde Farm at Cutnall Green in Worcestershire. It was to be his home for the rest of his life.

January–July. Recording of Houses of the Holy at Electric Lady Studios in New York and Olympic in London.

February. Led Zeppelin refused entry to Singapore because of the length of their hair.

Tour of Australia. On the return journey, Page and Plant record with The Bombay Symphony Orchestra.

May/June. Tour of America playing to an audience of 16,000 people at The Nassau Colliseum, Long Island.

September/October. Tour of Japan, Denmark, Holland and Switzerland.

November. Twenty-four city tour of the UK, including five in Scotland, plus a concert in Montreaux, Switzerland.

1973

January. UK tour.

March/April Tour of Europe and Scandinavia.

28 March 28th. Houses of the Holy released, entering the UK charts at number one.

May. Tour of the USA.
At 56,800 people, the concert at Tampa Florida breaks the record for largest audience attendance, held by The Beatles for their Shea Stadium concert.

July. Return to America for concerts, and to film shows at Madison Square Gardens for *The Song Remains the Same*.

August. Tour of America including two sell-out shows at Madison Square Gardens.

November. Jimmy Page records the soundtrack to the Kenneth Anger film *Lucifer Rising*.
Work starts on Physical Graffiti and continues until December 1974. (Recorded at Headley Grange, Olympic, Island and Electric Lady)

1974

January. Recording at Headley Grange.

February. Concerts in America including Madison Square Gardens.

14 February. Jimmy Page joins Roy Harper on stage at The Rainbow in London around the time of the release

of Harper's album 'Valentine'. Also in the band that night were Keith Moon, Ronnie Lane and Max Middleton.
Robert Plant and John Bonham (on guitar and looning) joined in at the end of the concert.

May. Swan Song Records – Led Zeppelin's own record label launched in New York.
(There were plans to release albums by Roy Harper, Bad Company, and Maggie Bell as well as Zeppelin themselves.)
The UK launch came in November with a much publicised party at Chislehurst Caves, attended by many of the label musicians. 'Silk Torpedo' by The Pretty Things released that month.

August. John Paul Jones plays with Roy Harper at a free concert in Hyde Park London.

In 1974 John Bonham appears in a film called *Son of Dracula* produced by Ringo Starr for Apple. It was directed by Freddie Francis with Bonham playing the part of a musician, alongside Keith Moon and Peter Frampton. The film starred Harry Nilsson.
Bonham plays drums on a song called 'At My Front Door'.

14 September. John Bonham and Jimmy Page jam with Neil Young at Quaglilino's Restaurant in London after a show at Wembley Stadium featuring Joni Mitchell, C. S.N. & Y and The Band.

1975

January. Concerts in Belgium and Holland.

February. Tour of USA. There were riots at the concert at Greensboro, North Carolina.

25 February. 'Physical Graffiti', the first double album and the sixth from the band, is released. (It took 18 months to make.)

March. Concerts in America.

May. Led Zeppelin play three nights at Earls Court in London. (The most expensive tickets were £2.50.)

August. Robert Plant and his wife Maureen are injured in a car crash on the island of Rhodes.
The band members become tax exiles in Jersey.

November. Recording for the next album (Prescence) commences in Munich with Robert Plant in a wheel-chair.

In 1975 Jimmy Page and John Bonham contributed to the Maggie Bell album 'Suicide Sal'

1976

31 March. 'Prescence' released, and goes to number one in the second week.

May. Plant and Page join Bad Company on stage in America.

September. John Bonham records an entirely percussive track in Switzerland with additional synthesised effects produced by Jimmy Page.

October. The film premiere of *The Song Remains the Same* in New York, and release of the soundtrack album.

4 November. UK film premiere, and the soundtrack goes to number one in the album charts.

In 1976 in the *NME* Readers' Poll, Robert Plant was voted best male singer, Led Zeppelin best group and Bonham was voted number two drummer behind Keith Moon. Jimmy Page was voted best guitarist and producer, and 'Physical Graffiti' best album (ahead of 'Queens' Night at the Opera').

1977

January. Jimmy Page and Robert Plant go to see The Damned at The Roxy in London's Covent Garden, and return the following week with John Bonham.

April. Concerts in America.

July. Tour of USA

23 July. John Bonham, Richard Cole and John Bindon are charged with assault against an employee of Bill Graham in California. They are released on bail and then given suspended sentences in February 1978.

The remaining dates of the tour are cancelled when Robert Plant's son Karac dies from a virus infection.

In the readers' poll of a popular UK weekly music magazine 'The Song Remains the Same' wins best album award and Jimmy page is voted best guitarist.

1978

May. Rehearsals at Clearwell Castle in The Forest of Dean follow a period of more than six months inactivity for the band.

July. Robert Plant plays a small gig at the Wolverly Memorial Hall near his home. The band name was Melvin Giganticus and the Turd Burglers and the set largely comprised of rock and roll standards.

August. Robert Plant jams with Dr Feelgood at a club in Ibiza.

December. 'In Through the Out Door' recorded at Polar Music Studios in Stockholm.

1979

John Bonham plays drums on the Roy Wood LP 'On the Road Again' on the track called 'Keep Your Hands on the Wheel'.

4 August. Led Zeppelin play at Knebworth.

15 August. 'In Through the Out Door' released.

John Bonham's last live UK appearance was possibly with Paul McCartney, at the concert for Kampuchea at Hammersmith Odeon London, in December 1979. Bonzo joined John Paul Jones and Pete Townsend as a member of the Rockestra.

He also played on two tracks of the last ever Wings album 'Back to the Egg' with John Paul Jones.

1979 cont'd

In the 1979 *Melody Maker* readers' poll, Led Zeppelin are voted Band of the Year, Best Live Act, and 'In through the Out Door' is voted best album. Plant is voted as best singer, Page as best guitarist, producer and arranger. Bonham is second best drummer, and Jones second best bass player and keyboard player.

In the *NME* of the same year Zeppelin are voted best group, Plant as best male singer and Bonham as best drummer.

1980

25 September. Death of John Bonham, aged 32, at Jimmy Page's house in Windsor.

4 December. Led Zeppelin disbanded.

1982

19 November. Coda released.

The following was taken from the Atlantic Records press release 4 December 1980,

'We wish it to be known that the loss of our dear friend and the deep respect we have for his family, together with the sense of undivided harmony felt by ourselves and our manager, have led us to decide that we could not continue as we are'.
– Led Zeppelin

DEBORAH BONHAM

It's not difficult to put into words what John and Michael meant to me, one word suffices – everything. I guess you could say that I've been blessed, because unlike some people, I have these incredible, beautiful memories, many of which are captured in this book. I've got that to hold on to. Still, I can't help feeling I've been short changed. There is such a void. I miss the humour, the music – we were all so like-minded in our love for all styles of music, I miss the discussions and the banter – the companionship. I miss them.

I had such an introduction into music at such an early age – 'Led Zeppelin 1'. I used to make my friends come round and play 'Dazed and Confused' and say, "Right, start dancing when the fast bit comes in." We were only 7! John's drumming always astounded me and the only drummer I can say has come close to him is his son Jason, who I had the pleasure of working with on my album 'The Old Hyde' that I wrote for John, Dad and Michael.

Without a doubt, Led Zeppelin's music has been incredibly influential to me. How could it not – I lived with it and I love it. I love the fact that you can't pigeon-hole it. There is such an array of blues, rock, folk and soul – each track different in style and each album different – something lacking in a lot of new bands today. If only record companies would let bands be a little more inventive instead of thinking 'radio formula'. Led Zeppelin didn't give a toss about that – it was always about the music and that's why it worked. To this day, I am one of their biggest fans. I've moved houses three times to find new people to play 'The Song Remains the Same' video to! It became a standing joke at our old house – we'd go down to the pub, have a few beers (as you do) then back to the house for a party. My husband Pete would watch me from a distance thinking "any moment now" and sure enough I'd utter those fateful words, "Where's me video – lets watch Led Zeppelin". For all of you who know the film well – the bit where

Jonesy and John look at each other during 'Dazed and Confused'. I think Jonesy wants to come in too early on an accent and John looks at him and shakes his head – I just love that. It just shows how close those two were. I've worn out three videos but now I have the DVD!! So I've moved house again and I've got a load of new friends at our local pub who haven't seen it. Joy!

John had such a great respect for many styles of music, especially Motown. Him and Michael regularly played James Brown, Otis Reading, Sam and Dave, Smokey Robinson, Aretha Franklin (to name a few). This had a big influence on me. They were also both into Joni Mitchel, CSNY and Fleetwood Mac. When Mick Fleetwood played on my album, all I could think about was when I used to listen to them with John and Michael, it had such a huge affect on me.

They say all music holds a memory for someone somewhere – and Joni Mitchel's 'Court and Spark' do it for me. I find it difficult to listen to that album without a tear or two. It reminds me of being with John in the south of France whilst John was on tax exile. We used to play that album all the time – John used to say to me, "Listen to the piano in that, what d'yer think – beautiful init." It reminds me of being in the car with Michael playing 'Help Me' at full blast.

I remember one night Pat was away at a Health Farm and John had asked me and Mum to baby-sit Zoe while he had a beer down the pub. Mum eventually went to bed, but for me, I was like a kid in a candy shop. John had every record you could think of. No way was I going to bed – I was only on the A section – I had the rest of the alphabet to do. Eventually he came home and said, "Oh, you're listening to Hendrix?" I hadn't really heard much of him but had heard a lot about him. John suddenly disappeared and came back with a load of videos. We sat up till the early hours watching Hendrix and the Isle of White festival and talking about every bit of music you could think of. It was one of the loveliest moments I have shared with my big brother and an evening I'll always treasure.

Buying my horse is another treasured moment for me. It's the only time I can remember where there was just the three of us, John, Michael and me. We had such a wonderful day together. The fact that the whole day was about buying 'Achilles' is now immaterial. OK, it wasn't at the time, but now I look back and think what a special moment that was. When 'Roxanne' by the Police came on, John turned it up full blast and said, "They're going to be the next big band." He was so right – he just knew a great song when he heard it. Needless to say, I became a huge Police fan, that was until John took me to see them.

The Police were playing the Birmingham Odeon. Don't ask me when, unlike Michael, I never kept a diary. I just remember John and Matthew coming to pick me up with Jason and we all went off to the show. It must have been late 70s I guess, cos I remember thinking how great it was that John still wanted to see up and coming bands even though Zeppelin were so huge and the Police certainly weren't.

We arrived at the venue and were ushered to the side of the stage. We watched a staggering show. The band was totally fantastic and as they came off, John congratulated all of them. We were then asked back stage to meet them. On arrival, John was so complimentary. He met with Stuart Copeland who was slightly in awe of him, and also with Andy Summers, both lovely chaps. They seemed overwhelmed that John Bonham of Led Zeppelin had come to watch them, and more importantly, thought they were great.

Everything was going well until John turned round to see Sting, who was sitting on a rocking chair and had a totally different attitude to that of his fellow band members. John mentioned to them that he was playing the Albert Hall in London for 'Rock for Kampuchea' with Paul McCartney and a bunch of guests and would they like to come down and get up for a jam. To this Sting said "Paul who?" and as John walked over to him Sting said, "Hey, don't step on my blue suede shoes."

Funny how you remember things – this memory has stuck with me. It's also funny how you can switch from group adoration to family loyalty in one second. All of a sudden I went from 'This guy is great' to 'This guy is a twat'. Paul who???? Oh please, he can't be that much of a Muppet.

Things got a little bit heated, but all the time, John kept his cool. I remember thinking 'whack him', but John kept his cool and we left. In the car on the way home, I mouthed off about how disgusting I thought it was, and who the hell did he think he was in front of such greatness. (OK you've got to remember he was my brother and the best drummer in the best band and in the world to me). John turned round and said, "You know what, we were like that when we first made it – it's only natural – the guy is going to go a hell of a long way – he's got an incredible talent."

Yeah, OK, but I still took all my Police posters off my wall in protest! Now however, I have to say, they rank in my top ten but I still have that twitch whenever I think of Sting on that day. Just shows how great their albums are to override that as I still play them regularly.

I'd like to meet him now to see what he's like because from TV interviews, he seems to have grown into a lovely man. I hope so. Certainly his music is brilliant.

After John's death, Michael and I became incredibly close, not that we weren't already, but there was a sort of great need for each other. He's been my rock and my greatest friend. He taught me a great deal about music and the fun times are too numerous to elaborate.

Suffice to say I loved my brothers – they coloured my personality and I'm extremely proud of both of them.

I guess it's better to have loved and lost than never to have loved. Better to have never lost at all…

LAST WORD

"Bonzo was the main part of the band. He was the man who made whatever Page and I wrote basically work, by what he held back, by what he didn't do to the tempos. I don't think there's anyone in the world who could replace him."

– Robert Plant